M000310255

—————— **Praise for** ——————

The Man's Guide to Corporate Culture

"Heather gives the best analysis I've ever read on how to become successful by embracing, and not exploiting, the differences between men and women in the workplace. Some of the best business lessons come from bad managers and so-called leaders—don't be 'THAT GUY!' Save yourself the headache and heartache—read the book and learn how to thrive in this crazy tech-fueled environment."   —MORGAN WRIGHT,
Chief Security Advisor at SentinelOne

"*The Man's Guide to Corporate Culture* is a worthwhile read for both men and women. It provides the tools and framework to understand everyone's perspective in the workplace, thereby improving efficiency and productivity across the board."
—PHILIP BARUCH,
Cofounder of DoubleLine Capital

"Ever wonder what to say, or not to say, around your female coworkers? Well, here's an honest take. . . . As a successful financial advisor in a male-dominated industry, I can relate to Heather. This is a MUST-READ for all men if you really want to know what we're thinking."   —KIMBERLY FOSS, CFP®, CPWA®
President of Empyrion Wealth Management
and *New York Times* Bestselling Author

"Heather blends scientific data and personal testimonials in an engaging way for MEN AND WOMEN ALIKE. This book is an easy read with important practical lessons."
—JAMES M. TRUSTY,
Ifrah Law Partner and Former Prosecutor
for the US Department of Justice

"INVALUABLE AND TIMELY. Enjoyable and practical. As a business consultant for many corporations, I know Heather is offering important guidance to men—and women, corporations, and, yes, couples, on navigating and elevating values of consideration, respect, inclusiveness, and healthy life/work balance in today's corporate culture."
—OLIN L. WETHINGTON,
Founder of Wethington International LLC
Corporate Consultant

"Every man should read *The Man's Guide to Corporate Culture*! This book provides simple ways for men to protect themselves in the corporate world. As an employment law attorney, a large part of my practice is prevention and corporate education. From a legal standpoint, Heather has formulated a great nuts-and-bolts source of reference."
—ANAELI PETISCO-ROJAS,
Chartwell Law Employment Attorney

"Heather's writing is as equally engaging as her on-air style—so, by definition, YOU WILL LOVE IT! She provides readers with logical solutions to complex gender issues ranging from the media business to the financial services industry. Her ability to synthesize information and make it accessible to the audience has made her required viewing whether on air or in print."   —GUY ADAMI,
CNBC Host and *Fast Money* Anchor

"The business world has shifted permanently. You have a choice—evolve or become irrelevant. *The Man's Guide to Corporate Culture* helps us men become part of the solution . . . not the problem!"
—MARK TEPPER,
CEO of Strategic Wealth Partners

"And finally, here is a successful woman who, from a woman's perspective, has generously written a guide for male executives and aspiring leaders on how to easily navigate the complex labyrinth of previously unwritten rules and obstacles in the corporate world during the #MeToo era and beyond."
—BRENDAN HUGHES,
Senior Retail Strategist, Gianni Versace S.r.l

"As a 'recovering' investment banker, board member, and media contributor, I have spent my career as a confidante to successful men, and what I am hearing more frequently is that they wish they had a playbook for operating under the 'new corporate rules.' *The Man's Guide to Corporate Culture* is that PERFECT PLAYBOOK, combining practical, easy-to-follow advice with a dose of humor to help you succeed within the context of today's shifting professional landscape."
—CAROL ROTH,
New York Times Bestselling Author
of *The Entrepreneur Equation*

"In the media business, I've seen it all. These 'Secret Rules to Successfully Work with Women' in Heather's book are a must-know to stay out of trouble. If you're looking for pragmatic advice and guidance on how to be your best in the workplace, THIS IS IT!"
—JOHN BACHMAN,
Managing Editor and Host of Newsmax TV

"This is the stuff that was missing from my MBA program! Through specific, relatable examples, Heather teaches us how to take a step back and reevaluate our behaviors. Let this book be your guide toward a successful career in corporate America."
—ROBERT J. LUNA, MBA, AIF®
CEO of Surevest Private Wealth

"Executives and corporations across all industries will benefit from the lessons in *The Man's Guide to Corporate Culture*. As an executive leader, I highly recommend that you implement one idea per week with your employees—not only will this open a dialogue on gender issues in the workplace, but you'll cultivate a collaborative environment for everyone. This book is a GAME CHANGER for the way leaders engage with both men and women in the workplace."
—JOANIE BILY COURTNEY,
President of RemX Staffing and Board of Directors Member,
American Staffing Association

THE
MAN'S GUIDE
—— TO ——
CORPORATE
CULTURE

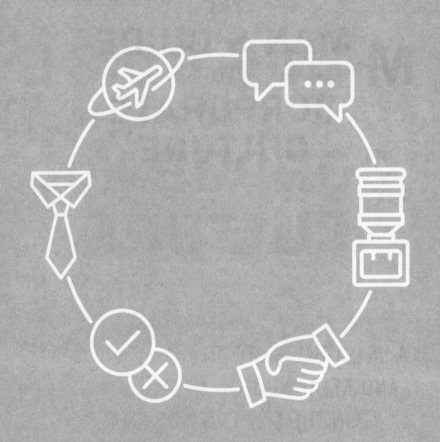

HEATHER ZUMARRAGA

THE
MAN'S GUIDE
—— TO ——
CORPORATE
CULTURE

A PRACTICAL GUIDE TO THE NEW NORMAL
AND RELATING TO FEMALE COWORKERS
IN THE MODERN WORKPLACE

HarperCollins
LEADERSHIP

AN IMPRINT OF HarperCollins

© 2021 Heather Zumarraga

All rights reserved. No portion of this book may be reproduced, stored in a retrieval system, or transmitted in any form or by any means—electronic, mechanical, photocopy, recording, scanning, or other—except for brief quotations in critical reviews or articles, without the prior written permission of the publisher.

Published by HarperCollins Leadership, an imprint of HarperCollins Focus LLC.

Any internet addresses, phone numbers, or company or product information printed in this book are offered as a resource and are not intended in any way to be or to imply an endorsement by HarperCollins Leadership, nor does HarperCollins Leadership vouch for the existence, content, or services of these sites, phone numbers, companies, or products beyond the life of this book.

ISBN 978-1-4002-1978-0 (eBook)
ISBN 978-1-4002-1977-3 (HC)

Library of Congress Control Number: 2020946657

Printed in the United States of America
20 21 22 23 LSC 10 9 8 7 6 5 4 3 2 1

CONTENTS

Who Is This Book For?

- Men Who Work with Women
- Corporations
- Small Business Employers
- Human Resources Department
- College Students/Aspiring Professionals
- Both Men and Women/Couples

How to Read This Book

The Man's Guide to Corporate Culture has three key building blocks:

- **The messages to men** fall into several subcategories: understanding the current environment (Chapters 1 through 3), toxic masculinity (Chapter 15), and advice/dos and don'ts (Chapters 4 through 9). There are two key chapters summarizing this advice: the dos (Chapter 10, "The Secret Rules to Successfully Work with Women") and the don'ts (Chapter 11, "The Seven Deadly Sins on the Job").

- **The message to corporations** on how to create a positive corporate culture is laid out in Chapters 15 and 16.

- **The message to both men and women** focuses on a healthy work/life balance, particularly as new technologies and the coronavirus pandemic have altered the ways we work together and communicate with one another. This can be found in Chapters 17 and 18.

INTRODUCTION

Double standards in the modern workplace.

I n the last few years, the national discussion around sexual harassment has catapulted to a whole new level. While it's about time that the spotlight is shone on workplace inequality, and steps are finally being taken to level the playing field for men and women, there has been an uncomfortable side effect.

The increase in highly publicized cases alleging sexual harassment against men whose careers were subsequently destroyed long before they ever saw the inside of a courtroom has left other men fearful of the perceived power that women now have. Many men feel like workplace rules have changed so much that the cards are stacked against them. They feel like they could be unjustly accused of sexual harassment at any moment for doing something they never knew was wrong.

Much like sexual harassment, these feelings lead to decreased work satisfaction, loss of productivity, and an unhealthy workplace culture. It creates unnecessary tension among employees of all levels and is a liability that bleeds into all aspects of a company. This fear is unnecessary, and I'm here to help men who want to be part of the solution, or at least not part of the problem, to navigate this new corporate world.

So, let's talk about this new power that women have and men fear. Working women are no longer afraid to speak up. There is a massive public platform to do so, and it's encouraged. In this new, inclusive corporate culture, women are eager to rise to the top. They are tired of hanging with the crowd at the bottom of the corporate ladder, and their new thinking is: *I can do this. I'm going for it. It's my time to shine!*

A lot of men are afraid of this new power, because they believe women can unjustly use it against them. If you are among these men, you are not alone. Even Superman is afraid. Actor Henry Cavill, who plays Superman, said that the #MeToo movement had made him reluctant to approach a woman "because then it's like: 'Well, I don't want to go up and talk to her, because I'm going to be called a rapist or something.'"[1]

What I say here is: *Thanks for being honest, "Man of Steel."* But really?

The feminist movement and rising whirlwind of successful women have shaken the foundations of the male establishment. What could go wrong here? *Everything!* Welcome to a world of confusion in the modern workplace where men aren't at the top of some Mad Men food chain.

Men's fears aren't completely unfounded. The courts are burdened with lawsuits filed by women claiming gender bias, sexual harassment, and other infringements against men with whom they work. While most are legitimate, some are unfortunately frivolous and absurd. All of this can be frightening.

Many of you men are afraid of mis-speaking, mis-stepping, and mis-doing your job. It's literally a battle for survival. You may also worry that double standards exist for men and women in the workplace today.

So, what's the trick to climbing the ladder and staying at the top when women are often now sitting on the top rung looking down (sometimes with a little smirk)? The reality is, the corporate inclusion pendulum has—for better or worse—swung to the opposite extreme and created massive confusion in the workplace, and you as a man must learn to collaborate and find synergies with your female colleagues, because women in the workplace are here to stay.

This book is a guide to help you do just that. My goal is to help you create positive work habits and communication techniques in today's inclusive corporate culture—from a successful woman's perspective. I will help you navigate the modern workplace.

After more than a decade of experience working in the male-dominated financial services industry and in the trenches of the corporate world—I might not have seen everything, but I've come pretty close. I've seen what works and what backfires.

This book draws on those experiences and is based around a collection of cases navigating today's inclusive corporate culture. These stories will bring clarity to situations you have likely already experienced. As these stories come to life, just know that you are not alone. You simply can't be "on guard" all day. Not only is it detrimental to your career, but it's a major health hazard. I want you to feel comfortable again.

Through real-world examples, experiences, and extensive research, this book will provide insight and ideas to help you work more collaboratively with women. It will help you to think differently, to not only survive but thrive in the inclusive corporate culture.

Of course, I don't want you to blindly obey a set of secret rules or ignore your instincts. However, this book will take head-on what's causing the confusion and challenges in your workplace and help you recognize the new boundaries between acceptable and unacceptable behaviors.

Not everything here will reflect how every single man or woman feels. But after working in and with various male-dominated industries—from Wall Street hedge funds, asset management firms, and investment banks to the fitness industry and media giants—these personal stories will ring a bell with most. After climbing the ropes of corporate America and interviewing hundreds of both male and female executives and colleagues, the consensus here is a revelation.

The Bottom Line: I am going to help you think differently. The feminist movement was for and about women, but it has irrevocably changed the workplace dynamics for both sexes. Guys, the truth is, if you don't learn to excel with women at your side, your career growth will always be limited. Women bring a different set of skills and qualities that your competitors are taking full advantage of, and if you want to compete in the marketplace, in the career race, and in the equality race, you need women on your side. And to do that, you need to read this book.

It's a Woman's World. You're Just Working in It.

The feminist movement has created confusion for men in the workplace.

Women now hold more US jobs than men.[1] So, let's face it, if you can't learn how to work with women, your career has no hope. This recent development reflects the future of the American workforce. The data confirms that labor market dynamics are tilting in the direction of women. Productivity and growth gains from adding women to the labor force are much larger than previously thought. A study by the International Monetary Fund finds that both genders bring very different skill sets and perspectives to the workforce, including different attitudes toward risk and collaboration, therefore boosting growth.[2] Studies also show that the financial performance of firms improves with more gender-equal corporate boards.[3]

Women in the Workforce

If you're not working in an inclusive environment, your company is missing out. Among other cultural issues, this is one reason the iconic Victoria's Secret suffered declining sales. At an investor meeting, the brand's chief executive officer, John Mehas, said it was ready to evolve. He wants the brand perceived to be "by her, for her."[4] But here's a problem: Victoria's Secret's leadership is predominantly male, and almost all the people at the investor meetings are men. Well, how's that going to work out?

Everyone knows there's more work to be done for women to achieve so-called equality, but look how far we've come. Slowly but surely, we're getting there. For us women, the dark ages have passed. We are living in the Renaissance for aspiring professional women. Fortune 500 executives are still male-dominated, yet there are a record number of female CEOs.[5]

In 2020, Jane Fraser became the first woman to lead a major Wall Street bank, Citigroup. Fraser's ascension to CEO is groundbreaking in the financial industry, which has a long-standing reputation as a boys club, where men dominate the upper ranks of banks.

During the pandemic, Clorox jumped 22 percent in sales when the board named a female to CEO. Marillyn Hewson led defense company Lockheed Martin; e-commerce giant eBay's success is due to Meg Whitman; and auto manufacturer General Motors survived because of Mary Barra. These women have all made it to the top on a combination of brains, brass, and savvy that equals or exceeds any of their male peers in corporate America. These companies are better because of these women and wouldn't be what they are without them.

Marillyn Hewson steered Lockheed Martin to the forefront of security, aerospace, and technology. She developed the F-35 fighter jet program to address modern military needs and increased market value to nearly $100 billion. *Time* magazine identified Hewson as one of the "100 Most Influential People in the World."[6]

Billionaire Meg Whitman is best known for taking eBay from $5.7 million to $8 billion in sales and joined the boards of both Procter & Gamble and Dropbox.[7]

And Mary Barra surpassed Rick Wagoner as the longest-serving chief executive officer of General Motors. She has the distinction of leading the US automaker out of bankruptcy.[8]

In another statistic, women now earn more college degrees than men. Women earn more than half of all bachelor's, master's, and doctorate degrees. This is a big financial benefit for women, because holding college and advanced degrees closely correlates with higher salaries, according to the Pew Research Center.[9]

Women in less visible roles aren't asking men to help as often as they used to, and men are less apt to offer, as they assume an equal level of technical competence in their female colleagues. Female upward mobility is an accepted part of everyday corporate life. There are fewer "firsts" for women entering new leadership roles, and it's a great time for women in the workplace.

Fear of Women in the Workplace

Given these new revelations: Are you a man who is uncomfortable meeting one-on-one with women in the workplace? Are you fearful of the coed office environment? Do you think a female coworker has it "out" for you? If so, you're not alone. You need to ask yourself how many of these feelings are tied to what's going on in the media and if you're doing everything you can not to be part of the problem.

According to a joint survey by SurveyMonkey and LeanIn.org, 60 percent of male managers surveyed revealed discomfort participating in normal workplace activities with women, such as mentoring and socializing.[10] These attitudes, while understandable in an atmosphere of fear, are detrimental for men and women and the companies that hire them.

> Sixty percent of male managers surveyed revealed discomfort participating in normal workplace activities with women, such as mentoring and socializing.

If you refuse to meet with women one-on-one, to hire women, or to participate in regular work activities with women, you're depriving yourself and your company of talent that half of the population possesses. You are missing different ideas and opinions—similar to how our government operates through a system of checks and balances by both political parties. A woman may give you that eureka winning moment of input and information that you never thought of before.

If you refuse to work with the opposite sex, there's no question that it will be impossible to learn how to coexist in this new environment. Your company's talent pool will be at a disadvantage, and the quality of your work output may suffer without a woman's point of view.

To avoid the appearance of sexual discrimination in the workplace—if you refuse to meet with a female colleague, then you will also have to refuse to meet with a man one-on-one. Does that make sense? How can you do your job without ever having a one-on-one meeting with anyone? Why not just leave the door to your office open (Secret Rule # 6) when a coworker, colleague, or someone you supervise is meeting with you one-on-one in your office? How about a transparent glass door? These are some ways you can get over your fear of workplace meetings with the opposite sex.

> To avoid the appearance of sexual discrimination in the workplace—if you refuse to meet with a female colleague, then you will also have to refuse to meet with a man one-on-one.

To avoid feeling uncomfortable at one-on-one business meals, a great idea is to invite everyone out as a group (Secret Rule # 3). This not only makes the individuals in the group more accessible to you, it makes you accessible to them. In fact, it's more equitable and allows everyone you work with access to one another, instead of playing favorites and fostering an appearance of bias and the resentment that inevitably flows from employees sniffing favoritism.

Executives in the Hot Seat

Companies have become much more active in enforcing policies around employee relationships. McDonald's Chief Executive Officer Stephen Easterbrook was fired for having a consensual and amicable relationship with another employee, even though Easterbrook almost doubled the equity valuation of the company in only four years.

Contractual obligations with companies can exceed the standards established by statutes and court decisions. For example, McDonald's personal conduct policy does not allow managers to have romantic relationships with "direct or indirect reports."

According to the *Wall Street Journal*, although the fast-food giant did not provide details about the relationship, Easterbrook said (in an email to employees) that his conduct had violated company policy. "This was a mistake," he wrote. "Given the values of the company, I agree with the board that it is time for me to move on."[11]

McDonald's decision to act may be a sign of progress on workplace issues that have come to light in the #MeToo era, said Carl Tobias, a law professor at the University of Richmond.

"Other companies don't always act on that kind of information or fire their CEO for that [a consensual relationship], and so it seems like they are trying to enforce a pretty strict policy in this situation," Tobias said.[12] While Easterbrook obviously did not violate federal law, he was forced to forfeit $22 million in unvested options when he was dismissed for breach of contract over his relationship with the employee. Talk about an expensive date!

> "Other companies don't always act on that kind of information or fire their CEO for that [a consensual relationship], and so it seems like they are trying to enforce a pretty strict policy in this situation," Tobias said.

And Easterbrook's not alone. Intel's chief executive officer, Brian Krzanich, also resigned over a consensual relationship after an independent examination brought things to light. The company, one of the world's largest makers of semiconductor chips, said that the relationship violated the company's nonfraternization policy.

Should an employer really be the romance police? Do corporations really have any business telling you (as an employee) who to fall in love with?

Unfortunately, clearly the answer is yes—especially with high-profile executives. Sexual harassment is no longer just about sex; it's about power and perception. Workplace romances between individuals at opposite ends of the power spectrum are sexual harassment claims waiting to happen, and when someone is in a relationship with a senior member of the company, coworkers will scrutinize every raise, accolade, and acknowledgment, creating a hostile work environment for everyone aware of the relationship.

Due to a change of heart, a previously amicable partner may become a jilted ex depending on how the relationship unfolded. Thus, suddenly, the narrative flips, and the company can become liable for the behavior.

Here's another case: ride-hailing service Uber has become a prime example of a Silicon Valley start-up culture gone awry. The company was exposed for having a workplace culture that included sexual harassment and discrimination.[13] That tone was set by Travis Kalanick, who aggressively turned the company into the world's dominant service and upended the transportation industry around the globe. The toxic culture at Uber, amid allegations of sexual harassment and troubling reports that human resources did not sufficiently intervene, sent up a glaring red flag about his leadership.[14]

These allegations went public and the company was slammed in the media for looking the other way. Despite Kalanick's incredible success and growth, the board of directors eventually relented to pressure and forced him out.[15] While Kalanick himself faced no specific claims of harassment, every public or private company is expected to define and articulate the culture and act as the standard-bearer for its values. This means, if Uber turned a blind eye to sexual harassment, the chief executive officer and leadership are ultimately responsible for it.

These men have added their names to a growing list of executives who have left leading public companies after details of intra-company relationships were revealed. The list also includes Google executive Andy Rubin, Wynn Resorts founder Steve Wynn, and Binary Capital cofounder Justin Caldbeck.

And guess what? Rules are being applied across the board. This new era is affecting everyone in power, regardless of gender. Women also have to follow the rules. The chief executive officer of electronics retailer Best Buy was investigated for having an "inappropriate romantic relationship" with a fellow male executive.[16] Allegations were sent to the board in an anonymous letter. The letter claims that Corie Barry had a romantic relationship with Best Buy senior vice president Karl Sanft.

A congresswoman from California, Katie Hill, was forced to resign after a claim surfaced that she had a relationship with a male subordinate.[17] Women need to play by the same rules that they helped create. Independent Women's Voice president Tammy Bruce notes: "This refusal to take responsibility for one's actions as women is a slap in the face to every person who has worked diligently to help women ascend the ladder of power."[18] Whether or not you're supportive of these new workplace gender guidelines, women don't get a pass either.

While most employers forbid workplace relationships (irrespective of whether they involve a direct supervisor), others may not take a position on consensual relationships, but that is becoming far less common. Even though we spend more of our time at work than anywhere else in our lives, it just ain't worth it in these precarious times.

> While most employers forbid workplace relationships (irrespective of whether they involve a direct supervisor), others may not take a position on consensual relationships, but that is becoming far less common.

The world's largest money manager, BlackRock, recently updated their policy on dating: "Employees are required to disclose all personal relationships with other employees; as well as personal relationships with employees of a service provider, vendor, or other third party (including a client)." Basically, anyone who conducts business with Black-Rock, not just coworkers.

BlackRock employs more than sixteen thousand people and services institutions around the world, who also have thousands of employees each and millions of customers. So, does this mean that every time an employee goes on a date with anyone who works in the financial industry, they should report it to HR?

In response to shareholder lawsuits, the board at Google parent Alphabet investigated claims of sexual misconduct made against executives and how the company handled them. According to CNBC, the company hired an outside firm to examine how its executives handled allegations of sexual misconduct. One lawsuit claims the board played an active part in approving a multimillion-dollar severance package to a former executive, even after he had been accused of sexual misconduct.

The *New York Times* revealed that Android creator Andy Rubin received $90 million in severance after several employees filed misconduct allegations against him. Thousands of Google employees walked out of work to protest the company's handling of sexual misconduct.

The trend toward more ethical corporate governance (better late than never) is good for everyone. Not only will the workplace be a safer place, but all employees and investors will be spared serious repercussions when inappropriate executive behavior causes the stock to crash.

How Did
We Get Here?

You need to know this, because it can happen to you.

I n *Curb Your Enthusiasm,* perhaps TV's most darling comedy, Larry David tries to tackle the overblown side of #MeToo. Through a series of misunderstandings—for example, using a tassel on his assistant's shirt to clean his glasses (without her permission), and grazing a waiter's chest in an effort to get food—David inadvertently ends up in a sexual harassment lawsuit.

It's important to know how and why we got here, and why sexual harassment legislation and company policies exist today.

The second wave of the feminist movement began in the 1960s. This led to many improvements, but it also led to many challenges. For generations, women fought to work and to be recognized as equals in the workplace—all of which are coming to fruition. This earthshaking rise of women in upper management has led to a new normal.

• • •

The Origins of Workplace Harassment

The term *sexual harassment* originated in the 1970s by a professor at the Massachusetts Institute of Technology, but it didn't pop up in general public use until law professor Anita Hill testified against Federal Circuit Judge Clarence Thomas in 1991. Here is a quick reminder of what happened:

Thomas was nominated to be a Supreme Court Justice. During Thomas's confirmation hearing, an official document surfaced about a private interview held between Hill and the FBI. Hill had worked with Thomas during his tenure in the US Department of Education and also at the Equal Employment Opportunity Council.

In her testimony, she described instances when he took her out socially and described graphic sexual encounters to her.

For women, it was a eureka moment—suddenly, workplace harassment was no longer a taboo subject. For men, regardless of how convinced you were by Hill's testimony, the career-ending potential of being accused of harassment was suddenly a new reality.

That's why it's important. After the case, the following year, submission and filing of workplace sexual harassment cases increased by 50 percent. These claims opened the floodgates to serious allegations—some real and some unfounded. Regardless, it put men on notice. It sent a clear message that women would no longer tolerate sexual harassment in the workplace.

Hill later admitted that she endured the abuse to advance her own career. During the glass ceiling years, this was often the only way for women to succeed—by attaching themselves to a successful man and sacrificing their professional integrity—but times have changed.

How Did Official Laws Come to Exist?

So, how did official laws come to exist? One more historical reference (*stay with me*): in the case of *Meritor Savings Bank v. Vinson*, the Supreme Court decided that women can sue employers for sexual harassment. In this case, the woman involved was Mechelle Vinson, who sued her supervisor, Sidney Taylor, vice president at Meritor Savings Bank. She alleged that he constantly subjected her to sexual harassment over a four-year period.[1] Her suit charged that such treatment created a hostile work environment that was forbidden by Title VII of the Civil Rights Act of 1964.[2] The *New York Times* summarized the landmark decision in 1986:

> The Supreme Court ruled unanimously today that sexual harassment of an employee by a supervisor violates the Federal law against sex discrimination in the workplace. Sexual harassment that is "sufficiently severe or pervasive" to create a "hostile or abusive work environment" is a violation even if the unwelcome sexual demands are not linked to concrete employment benefits.[3]

And there you have it. The concept of a federal violation based on a hostile work environment was a revolutionary one: no longer were women limited to lawsuits when the harassment was part of a quid pro quo for promotion. Now, even if the woman's position within the company is never adversely affected, the simple fact of pervasive harassment is enough to sue in federal court. And that's the least you need to know.

The Boundaries of Harassment

In the summer of 2020, fifteen former female employees accused the Washington Redskins of sexual harassment and verbal abuse. The allegations included derogatory remarks about physical appearances, unwanted flirtation, and touching. While these accusations clearly crossed a boundary, that's not always the case. Sports are very thrilling—especially basketball and football. As players celebrate a big win, they rush toward one another, fist pumping and giving high fives. While doing this, some teammates slap each other on the butt. Many times. And guess what? They can't do that anymore, since this is also their workplace.

Cleveland Cavaliers center Tristan Thompson was ejected from a game after slapping the butt of Memphis Grizzlies forward Jae Crowder.[4] Note: *butt slapping* is a boundary in your office too.

Most NBA and NFL players do not believe butt slapping is intentional harassment, or even an honor. It is irrelevant if you are sexually interested in the other person or not. What matters is whether the behavior is *perceived* as offensive. Courts use what is called the *reasonable person standard:* Would a reasonable person think he or she suffered harassment? You could be a gay man and be guilty of sexual harassment against a female (or male) employee. It does not adhere to the strict male versus female assumption.

The US Equal Employment Opportunity Commission (EEOC) is responsible for enforcing federal employment discrimination laws, enacted to prevent discrimination against an employee because of a person's race, color, gender, religion, age, or disability.

Stay with me. According to the EEOC:

Harassment can include "sexual harassment" or unwelcome sexual advances, requests for sexual favors, and other verbal or physical harassment of a sexual nature. Harassment does not have to be of a sexual nature, however, and can include offensive remarks about a person's sex.[5]

If you're still not exactly sure what that means, here are the two types of sexual harassment outlawed by Title VII of the Civil Rights Act:

1. **Quid pro quo harassment** occurs when a supervisor's request for sexual favors or sexual conduct results in a tangible job action.

2. **Hostile work environment** occurs when an employee is subjected to unwelcome physical or verbal conduct of a sexual nature that is so severe or pervasive as to alter the employee's working conditions or create an abusive work environment.[6]

Boil down all of these definitions and legalese, and this is **The Bottom Line:** Employees on all levels are being shown the door when questionable ethics pose a threat to the company's reputation. It will no longer be considered a "first offense" or a learning experience. Activist stakeholders are sending a sharp rebuke to brilliant all-star performers that competency does not put them on a different ethical standard.[7]

The Pendulum
Has Swung Too Far

The growing backlash in the workplace.

Finally, society is not tolerant of women being mistreated, but society may be more tolerant of men being mistreated and not just because it's less common. Why? You probably won't hear about it. Culture does not encourage men to advertise their feelings: organize a protest, wear pink hats on their head, or write a letter to Congress. Most men won't stand on the street corner holding a sign that says, "My boss makes me clean toilets." You just won't do it.

The Unintended Consequences of #MeToo

Tensions exist between men and women in the workplace: Who is making more money than who? Who was promoted because of a gender bias? Type "male managers" in Google's search bar and up pops "avoid female employees" as the potential auto-complete. It's okay to have these feelings. According to researchers for the *Harvard Business Review*, when giving critical feedback to women, male managers are especially worried about how the feedback will be received.[1]

> When giving critical feedback to women, male managers are especially
> worried about how the feedback will be received.

Male managers are increasingly fearful of giving low performance ratings to female employees. The chance of being labeled a "sexist" is so real that some managers just hold their nose and give the female employee inflated marks. Ultimately this is bad for everyone—the employee has a similarly inflated sense of worth (making accusations of mistreatment more likely) and the manager's false scoring is unfair and obviously hurts his team in the long run.

Some elements of the feminist movement have increasingly become based in revenge and anger. Misandrists have infiltrated and created terms like *toxic masculinity*. Corporations like Gillette buy into this premise and begin "virtue signaling" in commercials decrying toxic masculinity. This commercial kowtowing further legitimizes the hateful premise.

Media and news outlets have created a world where women have become increasingly comfortable in believing men are the enemy and must somehow be put in their place or conquered. This belief has backfired and is connecting the paranoid loop binding the whole dysfunctional landscape together. This kind of negative bias against men is taking a toll on society.

Even the founder of the #MeToo movement, Tarana Burke (not Alyssa Milano), said the campaign she started against sexual violence has become unrecognizable and misrepresented as a vindictive plot against men. Burke said that parts of the media had framed the movement as a witch hunt and that US politicians seemed to be "pivoting away from the issue."

> Even the founder of the #MeToo movement, Tarana Burke (not Alyssa
> Milano), said the campaign she started against sexual violence has become
> unrecognizable and misrepresented as a vindictive plot against men.

Many Americans may be reaching a boy-who-cried-wolf moment, where there have been so many accusations that they don't know what to believe. When someone you respected for decades is accused, it can be very hard to digest. And, in some cases, it's more comforting to disbelieve than believe, because believing victims may mean reexamining your entire worldview.

> Many Americans may be reaching a boy-who-cried-wolf moment, where there have been so many accusations that they don't know what to believe.

In cases where there are multiple accusations, it's harder to believe that many women conspired against a single man, especially when incidents happened in different places over a long period of time. However, women today have learned the value of sticking together. You reach a critical mass when accusations flood in, and it becomes obvious that there is truth to some of it, or all of it—as in the cases of comedian and actor Bill Cosby, Hollywood producer Harvey Weinstein, and USA Gymnastics national team doctor Larry Nassar.

False Accusations

I understand the destructiveness of false accusations. One day, I came home and my husband had found a large envelope duct-taped to the door with my name on it. I almost fell over when I opened it. The letter said I was being subpoenaed to give a deposition in a divorce case. My husband immediately began firing off questions (as I would). I had no idea what was happening or why I had been called to court. My mother-in-law was visiting, and she saw it too. Can you imagine how embarrassing that was?

It turns out, a former client of mine at a regional brokerage firm was getting a divorce, and his wife's lawyer subpoenaed me to testify. It appeared in his calendar and email that I had taken him out to lunch three times, seven years earlier. But taking people (mostly men) out for lunch or coffee is part of my job.

That's part of the sales process—taking prospects and clients out to lunch and talking about how various financial products might benefit their clients. My experience at the deposition showed me the depths to which people will sink to find dirt to smear someone's reputation. Four lawyers grilled me at length over whether I had ever taken clients for an "oriental massage" at work. Seriously! In retrospect (knowing that I was innocent), I was naive not to bring a lawyer to object to their crazy line of questioning. I would never take a client to a massage parlor.

My relationship with clients doesn't extend beyond the workday, but there will always be desperate people looking to create leverage by pushing impropriety into a business relationship. I know it doesn't happen often, but it can happen and it's horrible. False accusations, or even misplaced suspicions, now have absurdly powerful repercussions.

One way I could have better protected myself is by documenting the details of any business meeting held outside the office—a record of specific financial products that were discussed. Instead, my marriage was disrupted by a baseless subpoena by out-of-control divorce lawyers. Spouses may naturally assume that the fact that their partner is being dragged into court implies there is at least *some* issue to be concerned about with their partner's work relationships.

I had to spend time in a deposition where the questions themselves assumed my guilt—always with a snarling tone that seemed to make a point regardless of my answer. Here were two parties to a lawsuit, a judge, court personnel, and others hearing accusations of a workplace relationship that simply didn't exist—all because a wife saw "Lunch with Heather" notations on a calendar.

Unfounded accusations are destructive. I didn't deserve to be put through any of that, and I understand how it could have looked. It's extremely easy to destroy innocent parties by dragging them into a workplace quarrel with sexual overtones. But, given the nature of a sales position, part of your job is to be overtly social, to "wine and dine." If this happens to you (and you can afford it), bring an attorney to the deposition.

Men Face Harassment and Discrimination Too

Guess what? Men face harassment and discrimination too. The Civil Rights Act of 1964 protects both men and women from workplace sexual harassment. Women aren't the only employees who experience harassment or discrimination in the workplace.

A growing number of men are reporting sexual harassment—one in five of those who report harassment to the Equal Employment Opportunity Commission is actually a man.[2]

> A growing number of men are reporting sexual harassment—one in five of those who report harassment to the Equal Employment Opportunity Commission is actually a man.

Many men are targeted for their gender identity or for not being "sufficiently masculine," says Jennifer Berdahl, a professor at the Sauder School of Business at The University of British Columbia. She studies sexual harassment and gender stereotypes in the workplace.

Here's an example: A New Orleans construction company ultimately agreed to pay $125,000 in compensatory damages in a consent judgment ending five years of litigation, including multiple appeals, to a former ironworker. Why? The plaintiff's attorneys said the man was targeted for not meeting the gender stereotype of a "rough ironworker."[3] Can you believe it?

The following case was filed in the Southern District of Florida: Carlos was an accountant in Tampa, Florida. He and his wife were undergoing in vitro fertilization treatments to have a child. After each treatment, Carlos had to take intermittent paternity leave to care for his wife. When he returned to work, his boss assigned him their worst client account and male coworkers subjected him to comments like, "Want me to have sex with your wife for you?" and "I can teach you how to have sex."[4]

Another case occurred when a group of men came forward regarding sexual abuse that they had experienced in the military. It is estimated that at least ten thousand men are sexually harassed or assaulted in the military every year, and most of these men are young, low-ranking soldiers and sailors.[5] Much of the harassment and most of these assaults are actually never reported. As a result, many of the victims end up leaving the military with post-traumatic stress disorder.

Think about it . . . Laws at the federal and state level were created to protect all workers, but harassment codes were initially created to protect women. The implicit goal is equal protection for both genders, but it doesn't always work out that way.

> The implicit goal is equal protection for both genders, but it doesn't always work out that way.

Of course, there are legitimate, gender-based discrimination situations on both sides of the fence—women sometimes don't get the job because they are women and, less auspiciously, they continue to get pushed into the wrong kind of desk job merely because they are women. And it may take decades for some industries to evolve.

A Backlash Is Brewing

Depending on where you get your news, either all men should be presumed guilty until proven innocent, or every female accuser is just exploiting the system for fame and vengeance. There is a growing sense of fatigue around #MeToo. As more guilty predators are caught, so are more innocent men being falsely accused.

The "new rules" of the inclusive corporate culture have made some men afraid to hire women, including my former client Kennan. Kennan works at a New York bank and, after two recent experiences, confided that he is now reluctant to hire women because, "It's simply too easy to be crucified for an innocent gesture of goodwill." It's not worth the long-term career risk when the line being drawn can now include shoulder pats.

Almost any behavior can now be stretched into harassment. A poll by YouGov on behalf of the *Economist* found that 18 percent of Americans hold that belief, and that number is growing.[6] Despite the fact that few sexual assault reports are actually false, more men than ever believe that false accusations are a bigger problem than unreported sexual harassment or assault.[7]

> Despite the fact that few sexual assault reports are actually false, more men than ever believe that false accusations are a bigger problem than unreported sexual harassment or assault.

A study in the *Harvard Business Review* finds that not only is the #MeToo backlash not quieting down, it's getting worse. When comparing 2019 with 2018 responses, here is what they found:

- Nineteen percent of men were reluctant to hire attractive women; in 2018, it was 16 percent.

- Twenty-one percent of men were reluctant to hire women for jobs involving close interpersonal interaction such as travel; in 2018, it was only 15 percent.[8]

For example, a surgeon at a world-class research hospital in Washington, DC, told me that he was a victim of an unfair complaint lodged against him. After a highly complex and emotional lifesaving heart surgery, Dr. Smyth placed his hand on the shoulder of a female nurse and congratulated her. The nurse then filed a complaint stating that Dr. Smyth kept his hand on her shoulder "a little too long." He told me that she described the gesture as "overly friendly."

The hospital staff split into two camps and waged war during department meetings with the board of directors. Smyth was eventually cleared of any wrongdoing, but his reputation forever was tarnished and he was relocated. His career was completely derailed. And all of this due to a misinterpreted shoulder pat in the operating room.

The Artless War on Men

"Under penalty of death, no man may step foot on Themyscira."
—Aphrodite's Law, *Wonder Woman*

In Chapter 1, we mentioned several executives who were ousted. Contrast Easterbrook's termination to Dennis Muilenberg, the former chief executive of Boeing who was responsible for the Boeing 737 MAX aircraft, which led to the loss of many lives, billions for shareholders, and destroyed the company's reputation. The board took over one year to fire the CEO.[9] Yet the guy from McDonald's was fired in one day because of a consensual relationship with an employee, and not one person died. Amazing!

When Facebook founder Mark Zuckerberg and Evan Spiegel, the creator of Snapchat, first met, Spiegel left the meeting feeling unsettled. According to a *Forbes* interview with Spiegel, Zuckerberg boasted that Facebook was working hard to launch a Snapchat clone, so Spiegel went back to his Venice headquarters, and on the desk of each employee he placed a copy of *The Art of War*.[10]

The notorious stockbroker Bud Fox quotes *The Art of War* to the unsparing corporate raider Gordon Gekko in the 1987 movie *Wall Street*.[11] Sun Tzu wrote the book more than 2,500 years ago, possibly in the sixth century BCE. It has easily been the most influential and authoritative reference for military strategy in the entire history of war since the Bronze Age. Its influence in the twentieth century extended to legions of armchair generals in the business world.

"No leader should put troops into the field merely to gratify his own spleen;
no general should fight a battle simply out of pique."
—Sun Tzu, *The Art of War*[12]

In other words, don't attack a coworker just because she upset you. It's just not worth it! Sun Tzu also said that "there is no instance of a country having benefited from prolonged warfare." Just let it go.

Author Suzanne Venker calls the feminist movement "a war on men." The difficulty some men are having adjusting to the #MeToo era is legitimate. For example, men lose more jobs during recessions,[13] the number of men attending college has declined at double the rate of their female counterparts,[14] and a record number of male CEOs are being replaced.[15]

For decades, women have outnumbered men in America's colleges. According to the National College Clearinghouse, the number of men on college campuses has declined by 8.34 percent, which was far more than double the decline in the number of women.[16]

In the book *The Campus Rape Frenzy: The Attack on Due Process at America's Universities*, many specific cases of injustice, exclusively toward men, are outlined. The number of judicial decisions favoring men who have been unfairly treated by colleges has recently skyrocketed. For example, men accused of sexual assaults were often denied opportunities to cross-examine accusers, the effective use of legal counsel, the right to present exculpatory evidence, and sometimes were even judged by the very person who was prosecuting them![17]

Why are our prisons filled almost entirely with men? Prison has always been an almost entirely male structure. More than 90 percent of prisoners are male. As a reasonable person, you are probably thinking that there are more men in prison because more men commit crimes. And you are correct. You may also think that most violent crime is committed by men, and such crimes are more likely to result in incarceration than other crimes. Also correct. But many of us accept these as truisms rather than discussion points. Dr. Julia Shaw, a psychological scientist, says it's time to question these assumptions.[18]

Taking it a step further, it's not just the perpetrators who are male. Victims of violent crime around the world are also disproportionately male. According to the United Nations Office on Drugs and Crime, 79 percent of homicide victims are male.[19] Furthermore, 70 percent of individuals experiencing homelessness in America are men, of whom 48 percent are unsheltered.[20] These are major crises for men. Why isn't anyone talking about it?

Let Mars Be Mars and Venus Be Venus

Men are from Mars, and women are from Venus.

Some say that men and women are so different, they must be from different planets. John Gray's book *Men Are from Mars, Women Are from Venus* popularized this theory through the title alone.

In reality, we all come from Earth, but men and women do have different ways of doing things. For example, think of how you may react to a particular stimulus in the workplace. And then think of how someone of the opposite sex might react in the same situation.

In Chapter 2, we delved into sexual harassment, but we can also focus on how cognitive gender differences tend to get men into trouble more often. Diane Halpern, PhD, former president of the American Psychological Association, has cataloged plenty of human behavioral differences. For example, women excel in several measures of verbal ability—pretty much all of them. (*No surprise here.*) Women's reading comprehension and writing ability consistently exceed those of men, and they're also more adept at retrieving information from long-term memory.[1]

Men, on the other hand, can juggle items in working memory more easily. You have superior visuospatial skills: you're better at visualizing what happens when a complicated two- or three-dimensional shape is rotated in space, determining angles, tracking moving objects, and aiming projectiles.[2]

Navigation studies show that females tend to rely on landmarks, while males more typically rely on "dead reckoning": calculating one's position by estimating the direction and distance traveled rather than using landmarks.[3]

What all of this boils down to is that, for most corporate jobs, the majority of men are at a distinct disadvantage compared to women or to other men who have better administrative skills such as: writing emails, managing meetings, or delivering presentations. These jobs are not about hurling projectiles. Even sales positions, which are traditionally portrayed as fitting male traits, are actually highly administrative and dependent on a more advanced capacity for communication. Industries are rethinking these ancient myths as women have become more established in roles that were historically reserved for men.

Furthermore, men and women are sexual beings (*duh*), and the sexual tension does not disappear when you enter the workplace. A man who encounters visual sexual stimuli has an automatic tendency to become aroused. According to a study by Emory University: "When men and women see sexual stimuli, a man's amygdala (which regulates emotion and aggression) and hypothalamus (which primes a hormonal response) are more strongly activated."[4]

> "When men and women see sexual stimuli, a man's amygdala (which regulates emotion and aggression) and hypothalamus (which primes a hormonal response) are more strongly activated."

While you do have a choice in what happens next after these areas in the brain are triggered—harassment, grabbing, rape, or just tightly closing your eyes—the initial response is purely biological. David A. Buss, professor of psychology at the University of Texas, says, "Telling men not to become aroused by signs of beauty, youth, and health is like tell-ing them not to experience sugar as sweet."[5]

Men simply have a stronger biological response to such stimuli than women. W. Brad Johnson, PhD, author of *Athena Rising*, says that men can do two things to help:

1. Remain accepting but alert to your evolved attraction triggers in the workplace.

2. Your brain comes with a frontal lobe, so use it! The frontal portion of your cortex is that highly evolved region critical for decision making, judgment, self-regulation, and the inhibition of impulses. Think of it as the "brake linings" of the brain.[6]

Our Gender Differences

Women and men have evolved differently, and we continue to be raised and even schooled differently and treated differently socially. There is already a mountain of evidence that there are inherent differences in how our brains are wired and how we work—regardless of whether this is genetic or developmental.

Scientists are discovering neurostructural reasons that explain why men are often visually oriented. That visual orientation is especially at-tuned to stimuli you perceive as sexual, and your initial reaction is more likely to be visceral, instinctive, and automatic than it would be in a woman.[7] So, you see, biology stacks the deck against men who work with women, right from the start.

Furthermore, Halpern says there is overwhelming data among pri-mates pointing to a biological basis of sex-based cognitive differences. In one study of thirty-four monkeys, males strongly preferred toys with wheels over plush toys, whereas females found plush toys much more likable.[8]

> In one study of thirty-four monkeys, males strongly preferred toys with wheels over plush toys, whereas females found plush toys much more likable.

Okay, so we're *not* monkeys, but these behaviors are essential for survival and propagation. "They are innate, rather than learned," says Nirao Shah, professor of behavioral sciences and neurobiology at Stanford University. Shah's studies indicate how some genes in the mouse brain determine sex-specific behaviors, like the female trait of protecting the nest from intruders. And most of these genes, he says, have human analogues.[9]

Acceptance of evolutionary adaptations between the genders is key to understanding the differences between men and women that permeate the workplace. There may also be overlap, and in other areas reality may run completely counter to the stereotype, but clearly there are two distinct biological platforms. While this book does not attempt to enumerate every difference between the sexes or where they originate— including genetic, developmental, educational, or cultural—we must acknowledge that there are indeed differences. Here are some of these key female differences that you should prepare for.

What Is Her Body Telling You?

An organizational psychologist, Dr. Jim Bright studies the ways employees speak with their coworkers, and why it's getting easier to offend people. It can be difficult to know what is or is not appropriate. So, Bright recommends reading the room and each individual before saying something potentially offensive. This is a skill most people don't have.[10]

Believe it or not, men and women use roughly the same amount of words per day.[11] (*I know you don't believe me.*) But, when it comes to body language, it's completely different. For example, nodding is an interesting nonverbal behavior that both sexes typically do for very different reasons. When a woman nods, she is usually trying to show agreement. When a guy nods, he is more often signaling that he is listening and wants the person to continue rambling.[12]

> When a woman nods, she is usually trying to show agreement. When a guy nods, he is more often signaling that he is listening and wants the person to continue rambling.

Our faces can demonstrate more than ten thousand facial expressions. However, men and women use them differently. Overall, women demonstrate more facial expressiveness than men—they smile and show more emotion[13]—and therefore may be better at reading facial expressiveness.

Most men want to be respectful of women, and you are! However, the way a woman dresses can be a problem. You don't want the distraction or temptation of bare skin, short skirts, or high heels to cross your mind in the workplace, but it happens. Researchers at the University of California found that, even in a natural resting state, men's brains are much more attuned to external, visual stimuli than women's brains.[14] But, telling people how to dress or commenting on their style can easily become a human resources nightmare. So, what can you do about it? *Stop it!* Look at her face. No, really. Try to compartmentalize in your brain the difference between your professional life and your personal life.

On the other hand, HR is not going to tell female employees they can't show any skin, or no one would work there. Can you imagine the pushback? You have to treat your employees like adults. If you're an adult and you can't deal with a professional woman showing some skin, then you should work from home. Men know that sexual harassment is grounds for termination, unethical, and immoral.

I'm definitely not averse to male attention and I'm not opposed to someone telling me that I look nice, but there is a fine line. For example, I've never told a male coworker, "Hey, your legs look great in those suit pants." When referring to attire, saying something like, "That's a nice color," is fine, but don't mention a woman's physical appearance at work. Unless you work in an industry where appearance matters (such as the fitness, cosmetic, entertainment, or media industries), that's a big no-no.

This speaks to the heart of the problem—men are faced with a fairly amorphous legal concept, "hostile environment," and with different levels of sensitivity by female employees. The safest route is to assume that all female colleagues may be sensitive or even offended by your comment. If three women think you're sociable and funny, that does not mean the fourth woman won't be offended by a compliment on her physical appearance. An assumption that all women have the same trigger can lead to an awkward situation for you.

What Is Your Body Telling Her?

The art of listening begins with being aware of your surroundings. Turn your body toward the person who is speaking, put your phone on mute, and minimize interruptions. Think about your nonverbal cues. What is your body telling her?

Men tend to exhibit body language behaviors such as side-to-side head shaking; a tall, towering stance; or sitting sprawled with their legs spread widely and their arms stretched out on the back of a chair. If you do this, you're sending a status or power signal to your coworkers. It may be an unconscious behavior, but it's not good.

> Men tend to exhibit body language behaviors such as side-to-side head shaking; a tall, towering stance; or sitting sprawled with their legs spread widely and their arms stretched out on the back of a chair.

A communication style can turn into a weakness if it's overdone. A woman's collaborative approach can come across as submissive, while a man's directness can be taken as callousness. Men come across as too aggressive when their expansive postures infringe on other people's personal space, when they have a "death grip" handshake, and when they emphasize status cues to the point where they look egotistical and uncaring.

On the other hand, women are viewed as weak or passive when they are unnecessarily apologetic, when they smile excessively or inappropriately, and when they discount their own ideas and achievements.[15]

Here are some things to remember:

1. Make good eye contact.
2. Keep an open posture.
3. Don't interrupt while your coworker is speaking.

4. Try *active listening*—repeat back what is said and nod your head.

Outside the workplace there are also differences between how men and women communicate through physical touch. Men use high fives, back pats, and shoulder touches as a way to display dominance. Men will use an introductory handshake to set the tone. Women may reach out and touch someone's arm or offer a hug to build a connection and show support.

Researcher Paul Zak found that touch releases a hormone in our brains called oxytocin, Science of People reports.[16] Oxytocin, the "love hormone," impacts men and women differently in the workplace. In men, it improves the ability to identify competitive relationships; whereas in women, it facilitates the ability to collaborate. This hormone is found in increased amounts when people hug, regardless of gender.

Comfort with the Opposite Sex

For nine years I was the leading salesperson at SunAmerica, a provider of annuities and mutual funds. I was the only female salesperson in the company, which provided me a unique perspective of observing male behavior in a corporate setting. As I excelled in an institutional sales role, I received the number-one wholesaler award several times. Every time I took the stage, I was the only woman onstage. It was usually a hundred men, and me. I'm not kidding!

During that time (while I can't speak for other women), I never experienced sexual harassment. I *was* bullied many times, but it was not sexual harassment.

> I am a "minority" in the financial services industry, but I've never viewed myself as a victim. I never believed that being a woman somehow put me at a disadvantage.

I am a "minority" in the financial services industry, but I've never viewed myself as a victim. I never believed that being a woman somehow put me at a disadvantage. Actually, being a woman worked to my advantage. To be crystal clear—I don't mean that I've used sex appeal to gain an advantage. What I mean is, there are situations where a male advisor might be more willing to meet with me and feel less pressured. If the advisor feels less threatened and finds me more approachable, I'm totally fine with that.

It's unrealistic to believe that you will like everyone you work with regardless of gender. Sometimes you just don't like someone, because you don't like them as a person, not necessarily because of their gender. But when it's a female you don't want to work with, there is more of a backlash risk should tensions escalate, such that the perception becomes an inability to work with women. If people think you can't work with women, your career will not last very long, and you could also effectively become more vulnerable to a sexual harassment claim. And that's a problem.

If you don't like a particular coworker and cringe every time you have to work together, it will be obvious to everyone. Trust me, she can tell. An "I have to work here to pay my rent, but I would rather not associate with you" mentality comes across as a superior attitude. It comes across as cocky. It's toxic. So, what do you do about this? If you're never going to like this woman, it might appear as a dilemma, but it doesn't have to be. Let's resolve this.

I'm not suggesting you run before her every morning and throw down a red carpet. You don't have to love her, but you have to get along. You have to act cordial. Not just for the overall health of the company, but for your own mental health and emotional sanity. An increase in team relationships yields an increase in productivity. And the more productive you are at work, the more coveted free time you have to spend with people you actually like (or free time to be alone).

The worst thing you can do when you meet with someone is to check your cell phone while that person is speaking. It's just plain rude. Please put the phone down at work. Don't let me horrify you by saying this, but your phone *can* be turned off without the world coming to an end. I promise. There will not be a total Armageddon.

> The worst thing you can do when you meet with someone is to check your cell phone while that person is speaking. It's just plain rude.

And once you put your phone away, keep your brain engaged. Think "present moment." I know it's sometimes easy to get into a zone or an altered mind state and forget about the people around you and your surroundings. *Is your fantasy football team winning? What are you going to eat for lunch today? How will the weather affect your weekend plans?*

STOP!

If all these things are going on in your head with the cell phone physically attached to your hand, you definitely won't even remember your colleague's name, much less anything he or she is trying to communicate. It's important to pay attention with all five senses, and most important, with your eyes and ears. Look the other person in the eyes (but not creepily).

One of the easiest things you can do to increase morale at work is to demonstrate you care. This can be as simple as showing interest in what is going on in someone's personal life. Companies like McDonald's are going out of their way to make people feel comfortable at work—employees can use an app that lets them adjust the temperature in their workspace.[17]

> Companies like McDonald's are going out of their way to make people feel comfortable at work—employees can use an app that lets them adjust the temperature in their workspace.

McDonald's workplace app has a temperature feature so employees can designate by mobile phone whether they are "too hot" or "too cold." **The Bottom Line:** To establish comfort with the opposite sex (at a minimum), you must engage in dialogue, and to do that, you must learn how to become a better communicator. (We'll discuss this in Chapter 7.)

Building Relationships across the Gender Divide

How to feel comfortable working with women,
and make women feel comfortable working with you.

Business runs on relationships. Building relationships is vital to your career advancement. You need to know how to get along with your colleagues. Your career is determined by how you relate to others.

In *How to Make Friends and Influence People*, Dale Carnegie writes: "Dealing with people is the biggest problem you face, especially if you are in business. About 15 percent of one's financial success is due to one's technical knowledge and about 85 percent is due to skills like personality and the ability to lead people."[1]

> "Dealing with people is the biggest problem you face, especially if you are in business. About 15 percent of one's financial success is due to one's technical knowledge and about 85 percent is due to skills like personality and the ability to lead people."

Can you believe that? Carnegie's book should be a prerequisite for any corporate job. Connections are the foundation of your career. If you feel like you've stumbled into the feminist corporate halls of glory, try to relate. Find commonalities. To succeed and thrive at work, it's all about relationships.

Investment bank Charles Schwab is a former client. The founder, Charles M. Schwab, was one of the first people in America to be paid more than $1 million per year by one of the most profitable companies in America, U.S. Steel. So, why did steel tycoon Andrew Carnegie pay Charles M. Schwab more than $1 million a year? (To put things into perspective, a worker earning $3,000 a year was considered middle class.)

Schwab's answer: "I consider my ability to arouse enthusiasm among my people the greatest asset I possess, and the way to develop the best in a person is through appreciation and encouragement."[2]

> "I consider my ability to arouse enthusiasm among my people the greatest asset I possess, and the way to develop the best in a person is through appreciation and encouragement."

John D. Rockefeller was the wealthiest American of all time.[3] He said that "the ability to deal with people is as purchasable a commodity as sugar or coffee. And I will pay more for that ability than for any other under the sun." Wow! That's how important relationships are.

If you want unhappy employees, there's no better way to kill ambition than to constantly critique and bash someone. I quit a high-paying sales job because my direct boss was not capable of distinguishing between constructive, and nonconstructive, feedback—he was always critical, never uplifting or encouraging.

Constructive feedback is supportive information given to employees to help identify solutions to areas of weakness they may have. It comes with positive intentions and is used as a supportive communication tool to address specific issues or concerns. Here are a few examples:

- "Hey, I wanted to check in and see how you felt about the conference meeting. Logan mentioned that you spoke sarcastically to him and said he felt uncomfortable. We need to function well as a team, so I wanted to hear your side of the story and make sure everything is okay."

- "I noticed you weren't in our morning meetings this week. I'm concerned you may have missed some important information. I'd be happy to go over what you missed. Then, let's work out a plan together so this doesn't happen in the future."

- "I saw a few numbers missing on the report. I'd love for you to keep that big-picture vision while working on these little blind spots. For your next project, let's put together a detailed checklist of your deliverables to make sure you're not missing anything. Give it a shot, and let's reassess from there."

All of these examples show genuine concern for the other person—tackling a problem without accusations or blame. Another good way to temper any blowback is to empathize and talk about your own mistakes before criticizing the other person and then share how you dealt with the same situation.

The Art of Small Talk

Small Talk: a moment of caring through words. This is an art, not a science. You must learn how to open the conversation, or what is called an "icebreaker." Engage the listener. How can you make small talk without it becoming a debate about the coronavirus or the election?

The key is to find commonalities (Secret Rule #13). If you're married or have children, talk about them. It can be helpful to talk about your family openly and often. Doing so can disarm potential misperceptions about you. A complex manager for a major investment bank in Washington, DC, often spoke about his family to me—showing me pictures of his kids on his phone and sharing his wife's endearing texts to him. Because of this, I never once felt threatened by him when we were alone.

If you don't have a family or aren't comfortable talking about them, open up about your hobbies and interests. If you're a huge football fan, own it. If you love cycling, talk about it. A woman shouldn't feel threatened by you just because you're a man. If you're tense or can't relax around her, she's going to pick up on it. A woman won't feel threatened if you share a picture of your kids or pick up the phone when your wife calls. It's when you panic and don't pick up the phone that we think there's a problem.

So, what are "safe" topics to discuss? You can talk about things like the weather, traffic, the stock market, or sports.

So, what are "safe" topics to discuss? You can talk about things like the weather, traffic, the stock market, or sports.

Ask others about themselves; it's not all about you. One reason I have successfully bonded with thousands of financial advisors across the country is because I know more about them than they do about me.

According to Craig Valentine, the world champion of public speaking, the word *you* is the most important word in speaking.[4] Have you ever heard a manager in an office presentation say, "I'm going to talk to you about the new software design"? Or, "I'm going to discuss our fourth quarter earnings results"?

Guess what? Nobody cares about what you are there to talk about. Your coworkers care about themselves. What's in it for them? Change the statement to the following: "*You* are going to receive a bonus because of the company's strong fourth quarter results." Now you have their attention, I guarantee it.

Unfortunately, not every employer has the ability to offer a bonus to employees. A vice president of planning for a shopping center in Philadelphia told me he had to present sales analysis to the store managers every quarter. So, in order to get their attention, he created three fun sales categories. He highlighted the winners who met the predetermined goals during each presentation. Here's the catch: a store could only win each category one time. So, every meeting meant another chance for a new store owner to be recognized. "This is the way I keep them engaged," he said.

This is a time to reach out, show you care, and establish rapport. So many people have a tendency in conversations to go beyond the point where anyone is interested simply to hear themselves speak or to show off how much information they have memorized (or how little). Also, every detail about your life is not appropriate to share in an office. We don't need to know that you floss at your desk after lunch. Think before you speak (Secret Rule #7). Ask yourself if what you are sharing enhances how others perceive you.

Forbes made a list of subjects never to discuss at work.[5] Here are a few:

- Negative opinions about others you work with or the company itself
- Your sex life
- Gossiping about coworkers, unless you are advocating for them at their request
- Personal relationship drama
- Illegal activities (*duh*, unless you want to get fired)
- Religious beliefs
- Crude, violent, or hurtful speech, even if you're joking
- Politics (don't assume others have the same political beliefs and ideology as you)

People like to point to women as gossips, but men do it too. What you may think is an innocent joke may blow up in your face. Gossip has a way of undermining the gossipers. Never gossip about others at work. Instead, say nice things behind their back and you will see a positive return. The veracity of the gossip is irrelevant—the point is that it's negative.

A friend of mine who works in accounting for a healthcare company in Minnetonka, Minnesota, was talking to a colleague in the lobby about a coworker who worked on the same floor. He complained that the woman spoke "way too loud" and that her personal phone conversations with family were driving him insane.

Guess who was standing right behind them while the two were spreading gossip at the watercooler? Yep, it was her! She was listening to the entire conversation about her. To make matters worse, she ran off to the restroom . . . crying. There's nothing worse than talking bad about a coworker, only to discover that the coworker overheard it.

So, what do you do if this happens to you? In this situation, the best thing you can do is to immediately apologize. Try to diffuse the tension. It's hard to come back from an embarrassing situation like that, so don't be an office gossip.

Next time, it's best to speak with your supervisor in private versus gossiping about the loud woman in the hall behind her back. If you're uncomfortable doing that—then calmly approach her when she's not working and sympathetically say something like: "How's your mom? I couldn't help but overhear. I feel like I can hear everyone in the office, and I just want to mind my own business . . . but it's almost impossible. Do you overhear others in the office too? It makes it tough to focus on work."

By using "I" statements, you're not attacking her directly. You are simply providing an overall critique of the office environment, not her. This way, she won't easily get offended.

The Value of a Smile

The effect of a smile is powerful. Amazon is known for going the extra mile to welcome four-legged companions into the office. There are more than seven thousand registered dogs who visit Amazon's headquarters in Seattle, with eight hundred coming in on an average day.[6] What a great place to work for a canine lover!

Of course, if your employer is going to invite pets into your office, clear guidance must be established up front. But the benefits may outweigh the risks. A leading pet-sitting services company, Rover, cites studies that show how dogs can alleviate workplace stress and increase trust among coworkers. Jovana Teodorovic, Rover's head of culture, says: "While having dogs at the office brings obvious playfulness and endless wagging tails, it also heightens employees' emotional intelligence, helping them feel more comfortable opening up with one another."[7] Whether or not your pet is really smiling doesn't matter. In the human world, smiles are contagious. So, if a person looks at a dog in the office and translates its expression as a smile, it's likely that person will smile back.

> "While having dogs at the office brings obvious playfulness and endless wagging tails, it also heightens employees' emotional intelligence, helping them feel more comfortable opening up with one another."

Scientists have found that the concentration of happiness hormones, including oxytocin, dopamine, serotonin, and endorphin, increases in people after a positive interaction with a colleague—the same way it does with a dog. Research shows that you can elevate oxytocin (remember, it's the "love hormone") by listening closely to others, encouraging others, and complimenting others. This will also build trust.

The most consistent attribute of great leaders isn't brash assertiveness; it's empathy. These are the people who can best create a low-stress environment. Smiling and laughing can be contagious in the office, and can create an environment that brings coworkers together to interact in a natural way. This creates an environment where men and women can interact in a nonthreatening way that won't be misconstrued as inappropriate.

The sales manager of a large department store in Tysons Corner, Virginia, told me he would rather hire a salesperson who smiled than someone with a college degree and a bad attitude.

In a prior financial sales job, I made fifty cold calls per day and I always smiled as I spoke on the phone. Although they couldn't physically see me, a warm smile was still felt by the other party through my voice.

It takes a greater number of muscles to frown than it does to smile.[8] So, why exert more effort? *Smile.* It takes an estimated sixty-two muscles to frown and only fourteen to smile. When you smile, you're actually conserving energy. According to NBC News, "Smiling can trick your brain into happiness—and boost your health. A smile spurs a powerful chemical reaction in the brain that can make you feel happier."[9]

> "Smiling can trick your brain into happiness—and boost your health. A smile spurs a powerful chemical reaction in the brain that can make you feel happier."

As Dr. Isha Gupta, a neurologist, explains:

A smile spurs a chemical reaction in the brain, releasing certain hormones including dopamine and serotonin. Dopamine increases our feelings of happiness. Serotonin release is associated with reduced stress. Low levels of serotonin are associated with depression and aggression. Low levels of dopamine are also associated with depression.[10]

So, if you're not happy, fake it till you make it. Smiling, like greeting everyone at work, establishes you as a friendly and helpful colleague. It doesn't cost you anything and creates a positive impression with everyone at the office.

The Business Meal

A business meal is a leader's secret weapon. Business meals may be worth a dozen meetings in any other setting. Why? Because sitting across the table from someone is an escape from the stuffy office setting. It helps put your colleagues at ease. And it also may put you at ease.

As a female salesperson, I have lunch and dinner with many male colleagues and clients. In fact, if the men I work with refuse to eat with me, I'd have a tough time doing my job. Most women have no sinister agenda. Eating out can be a wonderful way to forge business relationships, to close the next big deal, or to network.

> Most women have no sinister agenda. Eating out can be a wonderful way to forge business relationships, to close the next big deal, or to network.

A business meal can also be a chance to bridge the gap with a rival. Richard Branson, the founder of Virgin Atlantic, told the *Wall Street Journal*: "Years ago, British Airways went to extraordinary lengths to put us out of business. But after the court case, I rang up Sir Colin Marshall, who ran British Airways, and said, 'Would you like to come out for lunch?' And we had a delightful lunch at my house in London and became friends and buried the hatchet."[11]

When you're at a business function, don't hold the chair for others (regardless of gender), unless they're in a wheelchair or on crutches. When in doubt, ask, "Would you like me to get the chair for you?" Problem solved. This is a very good way to avoid any misunderstandings.

At the end of the meal, when the time comes for the check, who pays the bill? It's simple: the person who does the inviting pays for the meal. This rule always works in the modern workplace, and if you're still unsure, ask yourself if you would do it for a guy. If the answer is no, don't do it.

> The person who does the inviting pays for the meal.

As I said, part of my day job is to take clients (mainly men) to lunch. And I always pay. It's expected. I don't grab the bill and yell, "Equality!" If a woman invites you or you are her client, just let her do the honors and accept it. It will save you money too. If you're not comfortable with that, you can offer to split the bill. It's a nice gesture, safe and nonintrusive.

Last, if it's avoidable, don't *side-sit* at the table with a colleague one-on-one. This is where you sit at a right angle to someone at the table, which sometimes looks a little too close. (If you're not sure what side-sitting is, watch *Curb Your Enthusiasm*.) Sit across from your female colleague, not next to her.

Awkward Situations

Work can be a marathon of mishaps. While every employee experiences some form of awkwardness in the workplace, not everyone knows how to emerge unscathed. A LeanIn.org and SurveyMonkey online poll found that senior-level men are nine times more hesitant to travel with women one-on-one for work than with a junior-level man.[12]

> Senior-level men are nine times more hesitant to travel with women one-on-one for work than with a junior-level man.

Well, *duh*. I'm sure you can think of a million reasons why: sharing the back seat of an Uber ride after a couple glasses of wine on a late-night flight, waiting in line to check into the hotel together, and then stepping aboard the confined, quiet elevator ride with bodies facing forward, and hands planted firmly by your side (like a statue). Can you say *awkward*?

The Bottom Line: If it feels wrong, it probably is. Here are the most uncomfortable workplace situations for women (please try not to do any of these):

- Making comments about personal, intimate activities
- Bragging about your accomplishments
- Making jokes about a coworker's appearance
- Giving an uninvited shoulder massage
- Staring below the neckline when conversing[13]

A lot of these situations involve invading someone's personal space. One woman told me that a male boss patted the top of her head when he walked past her desk. I remember a manager who grabbed my shoulder whenever he wanted something done. A man who works as a hotel concierge told me that he shrinks away from a colleague's hug.

Despite all of this, I've recently witnessed a decrease of social touching in the workplace—part of this is due to the #MeToo movement and part of this is due to social distancing post-coronavirus. We live in a technology-focused, socially disconnected world, where many coworkers communicate virtually rather than face-to-face. (See Chapter 18.) This means that we are touching one another much less than we used to.

Furthermore, personal greeting conventions are different in other cultures, and it's important to respect personal space (Secret Rule #2). Many Europeans are comfortable hugging and kissing cheeks during a greeting, but one in four adults avoids a colleague because of the way that person greets people. Three out of four employees would support a ban on physical contact in the workplace.

> Three out of four employees would support a ban on physical contact in the workplace.

My biggest client was an investment banker from France. Every time we met, we exchanged the double-cheek air kiss—a kiss on each cheek, alternating sides. But during our first encounter, I wasn't aware of his customary greeting. After the first air kiss, I did not turn my face, and yep, you guessed it—he accidentally kissed me on the mouth. Oops. Can you say awkward?

During the coronavirus outbreak, I remember thinking to myself . . . *Well, that's never going to happen again if we're all wearing masks.* Regardless, it's important to be sensitive to the conventions of the people you're working with both inside and outside your office. I recommend that you err on the restrained side in personal greetings with clients or coworkers whom you do not see on a day-to-day basis. **The Bottom Line:** Avoid hugging a coworker who isn't your friend, and don't pat a colleague on the head if you need a favor.

Surviving and Thriving with a Female Boss

How to successfully work for a woman.

know what you're thinking: *I don't need two wives to listen to, I already have one at home.* But your struggle working for a woman is a different type of struggle than your home life. In general, employees don't like being bossed around. But that feeling may be intensified if it's coming from a woman. No one wants to work for a boss who makes them uncomfortable or is a pain in the butt. You want to enjoy your relationship with your boss.

A survey of a thousand employees suggests that only 13 percent of men preferred working for a female boss and 54 percent were neutral toward the question.[1] While the majority of respondents said they work equally well with both male and female bosses, I think it comes down to personality and management styles, not necessarily gender.

I've welcomed a hands-off boss my entire professional career. My independent nature made me uncomfortable working for a manager who hovered over my every move. I just need to know the expectations and have the resources to get the job done, and then I do it. Interestingly, the survey reflected this same autonomous feeling for men, while most women preferred a more attentive management style.

In the classic *The Republic*, Plato advocated that women possess "natural capacities" that are equal to men for governing and defending ancient Greece. However (as you can imagine), many disagreed with Plato's views. When the women of ancient Rome staged a massive protest, Roman Consul Marcus Porcius Cato professed, "As soon as they begin to be your equals, they will have become your superiors!" Is this how you feel?[2]

The perception of what an executive should look like has changed. And these days, it can be a woman in a dress. Women make up more than 50 percent of the college-educated labor force.[3] Like women who lived in ancient Rome, many of us were raised in an environment where men held the vast majority of power and held virtually all senior executive positions. While there is still a lot of room for improvement, a lot has changed since then.

| Women make up more than 50 percent of the college-educated labor force.

The *Washington Post* reported that, for the first time in history, women now hold nearly 27 percent of board seats in companies that are part of the S&P 500 index.[4] That means men still hold nearly three-quarters of all board seats.[5] Men still dominate the upper levels of American business and politics, and I realize that. But there are a lot more women working for men—and men now working for women—standing by as equal partners, more than ever before. And so, "fear" of working for a female boss has increased.

| For the first time in history, women now hold nearly 27 percent of board seats in companies that are part of the S&P 500 index.

A friend of mine, Carl, worked for the federal government in Atlanta. He found himself caught up in a reduction in force, or RIF.

The span of Carl's career started at the lowest salaried position possible all the way up to a senior management–level position, which he held for several years. As he climbed the ranks, he was eventually assigned a new supervisor, a woman.

Carl never, ever had a bad performance evaluation. In fact, his evaluations were always at the highest level possible. After the RIF and an urgent job search, Carl got a low-level "worker bee" position in order to keep working until he could retire. The kicker is that less than a year after the RIF, the new supervisor advertised the exact same management position that Carl previously had, and the woman who was hired lived on the same street as the supervisor. They were close friends from college.

Carl submitted a grievance stating that his position, which was eliminated in the RIF, was re-created shortly after and given to his supervisor's friend. However, the case was reviewed and denied. The determination was that the supervisor had every right to re-create the position and hire who she wanted to hire, but Carl knew this was gender discrimination on top of favoritism. Unfortunately, there was no resolution to his ordeal.

> Since men and women communicate very differently, it's your responsibility to figure out how your manager prefers to communicate—via email, instant messaging, phone calls, face-to-face, or text messaging.

How Should You Behave?

Given this power struggle, how should you behave? In *Business Insider's* "11 Simple Ways to Make Your Boss Love You," one idea is to tweak your communication style to match your boss's.[6] Since men and women communicate very differently, it's your responsibility to figure out how your manager prefers to communicate—via email, instant messaging, phone calls, face-to-face, or text messaging. Once you figure that out, keep in mind how often your boss wants you to check in. If you can match her preferred style of communication, that will preemptively solve problems and make your job less stressful. If you're unsure, ask her what she prefers. Ask her what she wants.

Don't present a problem without first trying to think of a solution—even if it's not the right solution, always present a potential solution to a problem. This shows your boss that you have thought about the issue and are actively attempting to resolve it on your own. If you want a promotion, impress your boss with your problem-solving skills.

If you're truly speechless about something she said, or upset about a recent performance review or a nasty critique, express gratitude for your boss's feedback and move on. Expressing gratitude will make her open up to you. A simple "thank you" can diffuse most situations. Chances are, if you appreciate your boss, she will appreciate you too.

Greet Everyone the Same

At the office, the best way to maintain cordial relationships with everyone you work with is a cheerful greeting and a smile. I start my day by saying "Good morning" to everyone, which sets the tone for the day. In addition, by treating everyone equally, there is no way that my attention toward any one person could be misconstrued.

For example, I don't greet a male or female, or my boss or senior executives, any differently than I greet receptionists, assistants, or the cleaning staff. The goal is to establish friendly relationships with every employee in the company, not just your supervisors who can help you in your career.

If your boss is a woman, do you greet her with one kiss on the cheek or a firm handshake? Answer: let her initiate. Kissing as a greeting occurs less in big corporate cultures than in smaller or more informal office environments. Consider your relationship with the other person and the setting you are in—I may greet a longtime colleague with a cheek kiss in his office, but I only shake his hand upon greeting at a formal team meeting, perhaps in the conference room. (Refer to Secret Rule #10.)

When in doubt, if you wouldn't do it with a man, don't do it with a woman. People from other countries who work with your company in the United States might greet with a kiss on one cheek or both. If you're meeting with clients, it's actually a good idea to participate in their home country's greeting to put them at ease. (See Chapter 5.)

> If you're meeting with clients, it's actually a good idea to participate in their home country's greeting to put them at ease.

What else can you do? Compliment your boss, but not on appearance. Instead, compliment her on tasks such as her presentation, her performance analysis, or her client review (Secret Rule #4). Some women say they don't want or need compliments. Trust me, they're lying. Some things have changed, yes, but some things never change. Although the hit series *The Sopranos* deconstructed romantic ideas about old-fashioned values, chivalry is not dead.

Mind your manners (see Chapter 14 on etiquette) and stay in your element. Hold the door open (Secret Rule #9), but don't go overboard with the "here, let me help you" stuff. She wants to feel respected, but not coddled. She wants to feel like a part of your team, but not the head honcho. This is a daunting task to remember, but I promise you can do it.

Essential Manners for Men

Etiquette isn't about a defined set of rules. It's about treating people a certain way. According to Peter Post's *Essential Manners for Men,* etiquette is governed by three principles: consideration, respect, and honesty. These provide the framework for defining every manner that has ever been formulated. Each of these principles is timeless.

#1 Consideration

Consideration is understanding how other people are affected by whatever is taking place at work. Consideration is empathy. It helps us assess how a situation affects everyone involved, and then to act accordingly.

We all have our own workload and responsibilities to pull. A female boss may have her home plate loaded during a COVID-19 shutdown; or the young, aspiring, fresh-out-of-college coworker may only have "book knowledge" and lack real-world experiences. Have a little consideration for your colleagues. Try to see things from their perspective. Put yourself in their shoes. You never know, they may reciprocate your kind attitude at a time when you need it most.

#2 Respect

Respect (Secret Rule #12) is recognizing that how you interact with another person will affect your relationship with that person, and then choosing to take actions that will build relationships rather than injure them.

My former coworker Harris would drool at any attractive woman walking down the hallway in front of his cubicle. A lot of men are guilty of looking at attractive women who cross their paths. Sometimes you can't control it, it's instinctual, but at least try to keep your mouth closed so the flies don't swoop in. It may not be an intentional form of disrespect, but your colleague may see it that way.

#3 Honesty

Honesty is being truthful, not deceptive. There is a critical difference between benevolence and brutal honesty. Maybe there is a better way to say something like, "Well, that's a stupid thing to do." While honesty ensures that we act sincerely, try to use a steady dose of diplomacy in your comments. There is always a considerate and respectful way to be honest. Tell your coworkers what you want in a way that will give them room to think and grow, rather than room to run out of the office in tears.

Acts such as staring at coworkers, talking down to your assistant, ignoring opinions, or interrupting your boss are not just rude and inconsiderate—these behaviors represent a fundamental lack of personal respect. If you have a critique, it's best to find a way to bury it between compliments, like a "truth sandwich." It may sound cliché and transparent, but it softens any blow from the critique.

Having essential manners isn't just the right thing to do; it can help you grow your business. Sean is a salesman at a technology firm in Redmond, Washington. He worked in the global sales channel, responsible for driving performance. Their goal is to bring in new clients to develop long-term revenue in the age of digital transformation. Sean told me he had been "hammering a prospect for nearly two years, trying to get her business."

After countless meetings, it dawned on him one day that he didn't know anything about the prospect's personal life—the things that matter most. So, Sean stopped talking about himself and started inquiring about his prospect's family and background: *Was she married? How many kids did she have? Where did she go to school?*

Amazingly, when Sean stopped talking about himself and started learning and caring about his prospect, he earned the client's trust and he got the business. It was that simple!

An easy way for you to show interest in your boss is to take a look at the pictures in her office. She wouldn't showcase them if they didn't mean something to her. Nine times out of ten, coworkers will have pictures of their families, interests, or hobbies in plain view. And it's obviously not an invasion of privacy if a colleague publicly displays these photos. So, ask about them.

The Bottom Line: As men, you get it most of the time, but you generally may not spend enough time thinking through how your actions affect those around you in the office. If you just think about your behavior toward others, your conscious actions will eventually become a habit. It all boils down to one thing—being thoughtful of your coworkers: considerate, respectful, and honest.

You Can't Please Everyone

———

"I'm not a solution to your problem. I'm another problem."
—Joan Holloway, *Mad Men*

While attending a networking event at a fancy restaurant in New York City, one of the guests was a female executive at an investment bank. She sat across the table from me and had the most beautiful pearls I'd ever seen. Her hair was perfectly styled. However, she had the most sourpuss look on her face at all times. It was a look that read: *I really don't want to be here, but I have to.*

This is an example of a woman you can't change. No one wants to work for a boss who makes them miserable. You want to like your boss. The best way to do that is to be liked yourself, or at least respected. Here are a few things you can do to gain your boss's respect:

- **Admit your mistakes:** It's very important to take ownership of your work—and your missteps. Don't make excuses to your supervisor for something that was done incorrectly.

- **Be a good listener:** All women love to be listened to. When your boss is speaking to you, make her feel like she's the only one in the office.

- **Keep your word:** In order to gain respect, you must be trusted. Without a doubt, your boss needs to know she can count on you.

Sometimes, no matter what, a bit of realism is necessary when thinking about changing your behavior—you can't please everyone. Just because you follow these strategies and abide by The Secret Rules laid out in this book doesn't mean society will cease to develop new cultural norms for you to navigate in the workplace. Some women (no matter what you do) will still feel uncomfortable and excluded. You can't control how a specific woman feels, but you can influence your workplace culture to reflect different behaviors that make everyone feel included.

Communication Is
Your Key to Success

Enlarge your repertoire of communication skills.

At an annual wholesaler conference, I ran into a woman I have known for nine years. I noticed that she had dyed her hair and I complimented her on the beautiful new color. A male coworker overheard me and said, "I was going to say that, too, but I didn't want to sound like a creep." He thought she would hear "beautiful hair color" and think "harassment!" Although I don't think she would have interpreted it that way . . . we discussed things he *could* say without feeling weird about it. In the inclusive corporate culture, it can be difficult to navigate what type of communication is and is not appropriate. Here are some guidelines:

- **Don't make it about you.** According to *GQ*, the first defense against accidental creeping is taking the word "I" out of your compliment.[1] Even the most innocuous compliments can adopt sexual undertones when they start with "I." Centering the compliment on how you feel carries with it a suggestion that you think the woman you're complimenting is doing what she's doing (whether it's wearing a pretty blouse or changing her hair color) for *you*. "I" compliments are unsettling to some because they can sound like you're telling the person that what they're doing suits *your* needs. Giving a compliment like, "You colored your hair!" is a lot safer than "I love your hair color, it's hot."

- **Don't comment on a woman's body.** This may be obvious to some, but you should never compliment a specific body part. "Your legs look great in that skirt" is not an "I" statement, but it's unsafe with coworkers in the workplace. Before you speak, imagine that you're facing a guy in your office. If you wouldn't tell him that his legs look great in that skirt, you shouldn't say it. Just to be safe, add "Bro" to the beginning of the sentence, to see if it feels right. Specific body part compliments are fine for people you're dating, but not your coworkers. Even "You look pretty!" or "Did you lose weight?" can be deadly in the workplace.

- **Stick to professional accomplishments.** When in doubt, a merit-based statement is the safest compliment you can give. A positive comment about a woman's work, like, "That presentation was awesome!" will go a long way. **The Bottom Line:** Most compliments in a corporate office should not be about appearance.

Women mistakenly expect men to feel, communicate, and respond the way women do; while men mistakenly expect women to think, communicate, and react the way men do. When women talk about their problems, men usually resist. You assume she is talking to you about her problems because she is blaming you. That's not true. We are telling you our problems simply because it makes us feel better. If you assume we are asking for advice and offer solutions, we will just keep talking. Let us vent.

> Women mistakenly expect men to feel, communicate, and respond the way
> women do; while men mistakenly expect women to think, communicate, and
> react the way men do.

A key difference is how you cope with stress at work.[2] When focusing on a project, introverted or less gregarious men may become increasingly withdrawn, which many women may not understand. You feel better about solving problems, and women feel better by talking about problems. Boys are often encouraged to choose highly individualistic and self-actualizing career paths: explorers, inventors, analysts, salespeople, athletes, and so on, and the corporate world is often ineffective in teaching men how to collaborate and contribute to a team. It's assumed that you already know.

Here's something that may surprise you: nine times out of ten, a female manager will have no idea that a male employee is disgruntled. Why? Because you don't talk about it and often she isn't looking for it. Men are not as inclined to voice concerns, because it may be perceived as weak. But it can be harmful to your career if you can't constructively and proactively discuss issues with your manager. In extreme cases, it can even lead to emotional burnouts or meltdowns.

It's Not What You Say, It's How You Say It

How you say something is equally as important as what you say. The tone of your voice matters. The phrase "thanks for joining us" can communicate completely different things depending on the tone of voice. If you say these words with an upbeat tone at the start of a conference, it will show you mean it. However, if you say these same words sarcastically to an employee who shows up five minutes late for a meeting, it communicates criticism.

> How you say something is equally as important as what you say. The tone of
> your voice matters.

For most men, it's much easier to speak directly, bluntly, and get straight to the point. But most of your female coworkers and employees will appreciate constructive feedback in the form of a question with context versus a negative or accusatory statement. Here's what I mean:

Instead of: *Why weren't you at the meeting?*
Try: *Did something happen this morning? I noticed you weren't at the meeting.*

Instead of: *This plan lacks the necessary details.*
Try: *Is there any way that we can expand on pages fourteen through twenty-two?*

Instead of: *Why would you make the reservation at eight?*
Try: *Suppose our guests have kids at home—maybe they need to leave by eight?*

See? This way an employee doesn't think that you are questioning their abilities. If you rephrase the same question with context, it becomes nonconfrontational.

When considering how gender affects communication, keep in mind that with any human interaction, nothing is an exact science. Still, it is helpful to know when your personal "default" communication style (whatever it may be) is an asset, and when it becomes a liability. **One good rule to follow:** Praise a female employee in public, but critique her in private.

| Praise a female employee in public, but critique her in private.

In the digital world of texting, the inability to invoke tone and verbally communicate can also cause problems with statements or phrases, where your tone can be as crucial as the words. When handling workplace situations (if possible), it's better to speak face-to-face or verbally on the phone. Texting coworkers is impersonal, sometimes rude, and the greatest contributor to miscommunication. The meaning is lost when you can't convey the proper tone. Can you hear me now? Oh, you can't? I'll just type in ALL CAPS AND SEE HOW EASILY ONE GETS OFFENDED. *Oops, who turned that caps lock key on?* See what I mean?

And if you still can't figure it out, technology can help you. Microsoft's artificial intelligence researchers are finding their way into mainstream products. It can flag insensitive or noninclusive speech in Microsoft Word, and now that same functionality can accompany you as you write emails too.

This way, if you're dashing off a tweet and thoughtlessly use a gendered term like "gentleman's agreement" or "policeman," you'll suddenly see a pop-up notice suggesting a more inclusive term such as "unspoken agreement" or "police officer." If you write, "We need to get some fresh blood in here," the editor is likely to underline "fresh blood" and suggest "new employees" instead. Isn't that helpful?

Fishing for Compliments

Complimenting your employees will encourage them to do more for you (Secret Rule #4). Employees like to be complimented on their work. My boss is extremely effective in inspiring his employees through positive motivation. When I have a big sales day, he is the first person to call and congratulate me. And even if I don't have a big sales day, he calls to check in, offer ideas, and see if there is anything he can do to help.

During a visit to the White House, a senior official in the administration said to me, "I recognize you . . . you do really good work!" That felt good. Attention is a basic human need that we all yearn for in the workplace. A *Harvard Business Review* article, "The Ideal Praise to Criticism Ratio," states: "Only positive feedback can motivate people to continue doing what they're doing well and do it with more vigor, determination, and creativity." If there's a problem, and you can see it, but she can't—a compliment will get her back on track. Just the very acknowledgment of a coworker's existence can turn around an employee's morale.

> "Only positive feedback can motivate people to continue doing what they're doing well and do it with more vigor, determination, and creativity."

In general, women are more sensitive than men. Here's a quick story: Olivia is the vice president of sales for an insurance company in New York City. She told her boss, Bill, that she wanted to be the lead on a new life insurance plan rollout, but he decided not to include her in the high-level rollout to clients. Olivia complained to her coworkers about how bad she felt, but she never told her boss. She never even asked him why she wasn't considered.

However, Bill told me the reason he removed her from that rollout was because he had just hired three new sales reps and needed the company's "best and most talented salesperson" (in other words, Olivia) to train the new hires and get them up to speed as quickly as possible.

So, instead of asking her boss why she was removed from the team, Olivia felt better accepting a false narrative that she was being "punished" just because she's a woman. It felt better to complain to her colleagues about how unappreciated she felt, when in reality, none of that was true.

In her defense, Bill should have communicated his motives immediately to her. Instead, she heard the news from a secondhand source. **The Bottom Line:** Communication and appreciation could have easily prevented the situation.

The best way to raise employees' overall morale and level of productivity in the workplace is to tell them exactly what you liked about their work and why you liked it. You may be surprised to see that they're even more likely to repeat those same results in other areas of work. So, exactly what types of compliments are safe to give? Here are some ideas:

- **"Nice job on that presentation."** Public speaking can be intimidating, especially for a new hire. If you notice a coworker is nervous before a big meeting, seek out that person afterward and let her know how much you enjoyed it and learned.

- **"That's a great point."** If a coworker points out a solution to a problem, let her know. If you're grateful for her point of view, she deserves to hear it.

- **"You ask good questions."** Asking about something you're not familiar with at work can be intimidating. Clarification increases an employee's chances of success. Let her know the questions are not only okay, but valued.

- **"Thank you taking responsibility."** Accepting responsibility for a botched performance, a failed pitch, or a missed deadline isn't easy to do. Recognize an employee's truthful actions and maybe she will do it more often.

- **"You have a mind for details."** It's the little things that count. Details make a big difference at work. See if you can spot the smart, subtle details on an analyst's report or corrected client service emails the next time you're evaluating your employee's work performance and tell her that you're impressed by what you found.

- **"I love your enthusiasm."** Getting up and going to work every day isn't easy. Don't let her inspiring attitude go unrecognized.

Female Translations

Most of the time, communication in the workplace shouldn't be all about yourself. Believe it or not, people are not interested in you. They are interested in themselves. One of the best things you can actually do is listen. Not talk. However, women quite often say things that can be misunderstood at work. Here are a couple possible translations:

When she says: "Oh my! Did you say that you need me to finish the contract today?"

What she means: I heard you loud and clear. I'm just giving you a chance to change your expectations to reflect something more realistic.

When she says: "I'm fine. I'm busy handling the public relations project. It's a massive undertaking for one person."

What she means: I am overwhelmed or annoyed, but I'm not going to tell you why. You have to figure it out for yourself. Good luck.

While every employee has different likes and dislikes, basic knowledge of what makes women and men comfortable or uncomfortable is necessary. What makes them tick? What makes them happy, and what makes them afraid? This is where men must learn to read between the lines.

Unprofessional Communication

"Jackie, is that a gray hair I see?" Don't gossip about a colleague's politics, religion, or who dyed their hair. Just don't. If she gained ten pounds, don't start inquiring about her weight. Communication is good, but there is a professional way and an unprofessional way to go about it. Communicating professionally is Secret Rule #1. Unprofessional communication indicates a lack of respect for yourself and others, as well as immaturity, and it signifies a disregard for cultural and workplace standards.

CBS fired longtime *60 Minutes* producer Jeff Fager, who had been accused of sexual misconduct by former employees. But, according to the *New York Post*, Fager claimed he was fired because he sent a text message to a reporter who was covering the allegations against him. He texted, "Be careful . . . if you pass on these damaging claims without your own reporting to back them up that will become a serious problem." Regardless of whether the allegations were true, this unprofessional text gave the company a reason to fire him. CBS determined that Fager "violated company policy."[3]

Your texts are not as private as you think. Text messages can get you fired. If you're using a company-owned device, your employer has access to your texts. Even if you delete them, they may be backed up somewhere. And keep in mind that if you're sending messages from your personal phone to another coworker, these messages might be going to that person's company phone, so these records may still be accessible. Furthermore, anyone can take a screenshot or save your text conversations and show it to someone else.

A report by On Second Thought, an app that allows you to unsend texts within a minute of firing them off, found that 16 percent of one thousand surveyed mobile users admitted that they faced serious professional consequences (like getting fired) because of a bad text that they had sent.[4] And 71 percent said they had sent a message they wished they could take back.

> Sixteen percent of one thousand surveyed mobile users admitted that they faced serious professional consequences (like getting fired) because of a bad text that they had sent.

My Best Advice: Download and install an app like On Second Thought immediately and assume all of your texts can be read by your employer.

By enlarging your repertoire of communication skills to employ strategies that are most effective under various circumstances, you will gain an advantage. The most effective communicators are masters at balancing power and empathy signals so that they come across as both confident and caring.

The Humor Advantage

Some corporations are tapping into what I call "the humor advantage." Companies such as Zappos and Southwest Airlines have used humor and a positive, fun culture to help brand their business, retain employees, and attract customers.[5] You may forget what a coworker said or did, but you don't forget how it made you feel. I love to laugh, but gender stereotypes can affect how employees interpret this kind of humor at work.

Corporate conferences and workplace presentations can be very stuffy and uncomfortable, but some speakers can do the audience a favor by breaking the ice and telling a joke. Communications coach and best-selling author of *Talk Like TED: The 9 Public-Speaking Secrets of the World's Top Minds* Carmine Gallo says, "Humor lowers defenses, making your audience more receptive to your message. It also makes you seem more likable, and people are more willing to do business with or support someone they like."[6]

> "Humor lowers defenses, making your audience more receptive to your message. It also makes you seem more likable, and people are more willing to do business with or support someone they like."

The best speakers in the world are those who know how to get everyone in the room relaxed. However, sometimes a joke can backfire. At a tech conference in Salt Lake City, Utah, in 2018, Entrata chief executive officer Dave Bateman told a joke that sparked controversy. Bateman, the moderator at the Silicon Slopes Tech Summit, made a joke that some women in the audience deemed to be sexist—despite the conference's message of diversity and inclusion.

It went like this: He took the stage to introduce baseball legend Alex Rodriguez. But before he invited A-Rod onstage, he mentioned that his company uplifts women, and then asked the women in the room to stand up. As they stood, Bateman invited A-Rod onstage and asked the women to cheer for him (describing them as his "fans"), then told them to sit down and said, "Sorry ladies, he's taken."[7] There was a thick silence as the joke fell on deaf ears. A total backfire.

Several women said they felt marginalized and objectified. This is a classic example of a joke gone badly. But some jokes *can* be done right. Again, great speakers will usually open with something funny to get everyone to pay attention and shake them from the zombie-like state of disbelief that they are being forced to sit through a time-consuming meeting. Here is a perfect example:

During his keynote speech, when Microsoft's chief executive officer, Satya Nadella, took the stage at its annual conference, he couldn't resist telling a quick story about what it's like to work with Microsoft founder Bill Gates.

Nadella and his team presented the company's new hyperscale database to the crowd. After the demo, Nadella also said, "I must say this limitless, transparent scale out (cloud database) has been a dream for a long time. Bill Gates recently met with the team that was building all of this, and he sent [me] an email. And usually when you get a weekend email from Bill, you kind of wait and see. Do I really want to open it now?"

Gates has a reputation for sending email rants on the weekends, but Nadella closed his eyes and decided to open it anyway. "It started by saying, 'Wow.' I had never seen those words from him, never heard those words. He was really thrilled to see us make progress," he said. "Of course, he had a long list of things we needed to be working on as well," Nadella joked. And the crowd laughed.[8]

This is an example of a **Safe Joke:** Nadella made a reference poking fun at himself, not anyone else, and it's not gender related. Karen Edwards Kalutz, The Buckley School's director, told me that you can use humor in a business speech, but it needs to "boil up" and come out uncanned. Never begin a speech with a joke; work your way up to it.

The Bottom Line: If you're the speaker at a conference or an office presentation, make sure the joke relates to the subject of the meeting. It must relate to your work function and not offend anyone.

It's important to remember that humor at work is interpreted differently for men and women. People relate to jokes, stories, and information through their own lens—their own life situations and experiences. If you poke fun at yourself and your own mistakes, you should be "safe."

> It's important to remember that humor at work is interpreted differently for men and women.

What Women Want at Work

What do your female colleagues really want in the workplace?

In the #MeToo era, many powerful men are afraid to be alone with their female counterparts. A lot of men are outright sweating over it. You may be in the habit of compulsively micro-analyzing the possibilities of every word you say. How should you behave during office meetings? What can you say or not say to your coworkers without them taking offense? Do female colleagues see you as a threat or a welcomed member of the team? There's a whole gauntlet of new obstacles to deal with.

It doesn't matter how educated or how "nice" you are. Guys who once exuded self-confidence may now feel unsure. **Please Hear This:** If a woman is not comfortable working alone with you, you have a higher chance of being accused of sexual harassment.

> If a woman is not comfortable working alone with you, you have a higher chance of being accused of sexual harassment.

The truth is, you may very well be considered a threat simply because you are a guy. So, you have to figure out (and fast) what women really want in the workplace and address the often mind-boggling behavioral challenges that go hand in hand with working in today's all-inclusive workforce.

Automatic Data Processing (ADP) handles payroll for twenty-six million Americans. John Ayala, the company's president of account services, went undercover (donning a beard and mustache) to sit in a classroom for several days with ADP's new hires and employees. Why? In an effort "to improve the onboarding experience" and understand what the new employees' concerns were.[1] If you want to understand what women go through at work, try a wig and makeup (think Mrs. Doubtfire). But if you either a) don't think you can pull that off successfully, or b) don't have time, then read on.

What Women Don't Want

Let's start with what women *don't* want.

Apple TV's *The Morning Show* provides an interesting look behind the scenes of a morning news program after the male cohost, played by Steve Carell, has been fired for alleged sexual misconduct. In the show, Carell's self-defense is that the affairs he had in the office were consensual, so, therefore, he's not a rapist.

"I'm advocating for women by pursuing them."
—Steve Carell, *The Morning Show*

Make no mistake. Subjecting an employee to sexual harassment in the workplace is unacceptable. But some types of sexual behavior may not be as obvious today as they once were. Examples of sexual harassment include:

- Telling salacious jokes at work
- Sexually intimidating behavior
- Pestering or stalking

- Performing a neck or shoulder massage
- Unwelcome and inappropriate sexual advances
- Sexual stares and gestures
- Unwelcome physical contact, including touching, patting, grabbing, stroking, or rubbing
- Impeding or blocking someone's movements
- Starting rumors about a person's sexuality
- Sharing sexual photos or videos to a coworker
- Asking about a coworker's sexual history
- Inquiring about someone's sexual orientation
- Making offensive comments about a coworker's gender identity
- Asking about an employee's sex life

As you can see, there are many grounds for which you could receive a complaint of sexual harassment. Just don't do it.

If you want to understand what a woman wants, start with Abraham Maslow's hierarchy of needs—the human fundamentals. Maslow's theory is a motivational pyramid referring to the five stages of human growth. These five stages are: physiological, safety/security, love/belonging, esteem, and self-actualization. But these five stages can also apply to career growth.

1. **The Physiological Need** becomes the most basic need for employees to go to work and know they won't be victims of sexual harassment.

2. **The Safety/Security Need** is knowing that employees will not be ridiculed or embarrassed and will be allowed to perform the tasks they were hired to do.

3. **The Love/Belonging Need** refers to an employee being a part of a team, gaining a sense of belonging to a team, and being treated fairly.

4. **The Esteem Need** refers to the ability of employees to achieve their career goals.

5. **The Self-Actualization Need** is the awareness and recognition that employees did not achieve great success through random chance; rather, employees achieve success through hard work.[2]

A former manager told one of my female colleagues that she should become better at her current inside-sales job, because she would "never be promoted" at the company. He saw it as being "honest," but she saw it as discrimination. She was very smart and hardworking, so why would she not be considered for another position? Why would she automatically be denied upward mobility? The woman never received answers to these questions, but she resigned roughly six months after this occurred, citing this instance as one of her reasons for leaving.

According to the hierarchy of needs, the need for safety comes ahead of prosperity. If a woman doesn't feel safe with you, you're doomed. If a woman feels uncomfortable, she will constantly be on the defense. She will dig her heels in and stand her ground. So, you better start making her feel more comfortable when you're working together.

Listening to One Another

"A woman's tongue wags like a lamb's tail"—so an old English saying goes. Google's search algorithms can offer a window into our own collective prejudices. If you type "Why do women" into Google's search bar, the search engine will finish your sentence with "talk so much."[3] It may be a fair assumption that women talk too much. You may assume women talk more than men, like the female colleague who sits across from your office and yacks all day long while you're thinking, *Why can't she just get to the point and then be quiet?*

A veteran journalist told me that the most important skill in interviewing is *listening*. Being a good listener is critical to the success of workplace communication. What's the most commonly used phrase by women? **Survey says:** "You're not listening." Have you heard that before?

Maybe you actually do listen (with your ears), but your eyes and body are aimed somewhere else. Or maybe you just look like you're listening, and even nod your head, but if someone asks what your assistant just told you a few moments ago, you give a blank stare. Sound familiar? I'm sure you know of someone who daydreams just a little too much at the office or an assistant whose head is always in the clouds.

Through extensive research of both genders, many communication differences have been found. For example, men are more likely to communicate in order to maintain their status and independence, while women tend to view communication as a path to create friendships and build relationships.[4] Most men are not natural talkers, but communication from leaders and among colleagues is imperative to foster a successful, inclusive environment.

> Men are more likely to communicate in order to maintain their status and independence, while women tend to view communication as a path to create friendships and build relationships.

And it's equally important to verbally respond when a colleague is speaking with you. Try a technique called **active listening**. This is when you repeat back and reflect on what is being said so your coworker feels understood. Trust me, even if you're not really listening, the *active listening* technique (Secret Rule #11) will keep you out of trouble. If you're already a pro at this, build on your skill set and engage in dialogue with probing questions that build on her train of thought.

You can also enhance your communication skills by using verbal acknowledgments. Verbally acknowledge to your boss or colleagues that you are listening and understand what they're saying. For example: "Great concept, Susan. What can we do to get the ball rolling?" If you can't do that, then at least try a head nod and use verbal acknowledgments like "hmm" and "yeah" while she is speaking. I know you can do that!

Make Eye Contact

There are many ways to become a good communicator. And the most important way starts with eye contact. Here's why it matters: the ability to make good eye contact with others is perceived as being more dominant, powerful, competent, and honest. These are all traits you want as a successful leader. The ability to make good eye contact is a social skill that a lot of men in the corporate world seem to be struggling with today. It's actually a scientific fact—the higher levels of testosterone a fetus is exposed to in the womb, the less eye contact the infant makes.[5]

> The ability to make good eye contact with others is perceived as being more dominant, powerful, competent, and honest.

Need more reasons to make eye contact? How about networking with others, closing the deal, pitching an idea, making an impactful speech, or connecting with a prospect? Human irises and pupils float on a bright white canvas, but none of the other 220 species of primates have white in their eyes at all, or at least white that can be readily seen. The white part of our eyes makes it very easy for others to see exactly what we're looking at and notice when our focus changes direction.[6] And women especially notice this, trust me!

Anthropologists think our unique human eyes evolved to help us achieve a greater level of cooperation with others, which is helpful in building successful teams and partnerships in the workplace.[7] A lot of women crave attention, and the most important form of attention you can give a coworker is eye contact. Here are a few tips:

- Focus on one eye at a time and then switch.
- When you break your gaze, look to the side, not down.
- Never, ever look at your phone while a colleague is speaking to you.
- Don't overdo it—no creepy, ogling eyes.

As you increase eye contact with an employee, lean back.

As Michael Ellsberg wrote in *The Power of Eye Contact*: "In order for eye contact to feel good, one person cannot impose his visual on another; it's a shared experience."

"In order for eye contact to feel good, one person cannot impose his visual on another; it's a shared experience."

Your eyes are powerful communicators. So, even if your mind is on your fantasy football league or your next tee time, try to hold eye contact when someone is speaking. The trick is to indicate you are interested in what your colleague is saying without staring too long. Staring too long may signal a romantic interest or can even be seen as a challenge to her authority. **The Bottom Line:** Look, but don't stare.

Appreciation

Most women crave attention. Why else would we spend hours on our hair, makeup, and attire if we didn't want anyone to notice us? The fact that you shouldn't harass anyone is a pretty basic concept. But women also don't want to be ignored. Some days we need attention more than others. Our egos are fragile—both men and women alike.

My former client Robert is a financial advisor at a regional wealth management bank. He told me that he noticed his junior assistant, Stacey, wearing a fabulous new outfit. "She looked beautiful, but I didn't know how to tell her." Should he dare say, "Nice outfit today," or "You look beautiful"? Ultimately, Robert decided he would be better off (risk management decision) not saying anything at all.

Later that day, the team went to lunch at the restaurant down the street and his partner (a woman) acknowledged Stacey's new outfit. Her face lit up with gratitude and her cheeks turned bright red as she smiled ear to ear. *Wow*, Robert thought. *If only I had mentioned something to Stacey this morning, because I did notice.* After lunch, he felt horrible for not acknowledging the new outfit. I told him that a casual mention like, "Oh, that's different, is it new?" or "That's a nice color," should be completely acceptable. Ask a question. This way, you're acknowledging the outfit without any chance of it being misinterpreted as a sexual advance or as a critique.

Here are some more possible female translations:

Man (says): "Nice outfit today."

Woman (hears): "Well, what does that mean? That I don't wear nice outfits on other days? What about yesterday?"

Man (says): "You look so beautiful."

Woman (hears): "Is he trying to have sex with me?"

Man (says): "Oh, that's nice. Is it new?"

Woman (hears): "Oh, he acknowledges my existence." Bingo.

We all want to feel important and validated. This is even more so the case in an entry-level position where tasks can be mundane—repetitive mental tasks or difficult physical labor like factory work. Everyone wants meaningful work that fulfills a purpose. If you don't appreciate your employees, you will suffer, the company will suffer, and your coworkers will suffer.

Men in leadership positions need to pick up on this. Employees want to feel appreciated (Secret Rule #4), and your company's social media page can actually be an easy way to accomplish this. For example, Disney created the hashtag #CastCompliment. If you're visiting a Disney park and you have a positive experience with a Disney employee, you're encouraged to tweet about it. The employee's supervisor then retweets the compliment, along with a picture of the employee.

Disney Senior Programming Director Bruce Jones blogged about the program being "an opportunity to create some magic with positive tweets." So, whether you create a company hashtag or just make a practice of posting positive comments, social media can provide the perfect vehicle for publicly thanking outstanding employees.

Romance in the Office

Find love outside of the workplace.

Dating someone at work? The fact is, dating at work is a risk on many levels. It's an emotional risk to you, a threat to your job, and a risk for your employer. Despite this, given our biological similarities and differences laid out in Chapter 4, there's almost no way for both genders to work around each other all day and not experience some form of attraction. After all, not all office romances go south. According to a survey conducted by Vault.com, 58 percent of employees surveyed have engaged in office romances.

> According to a survey conducted by Vault.com, 58 percent of employees surveyed have engaged in office romances.

Sometimes, you just can't help it. Twenty-two percent of married couples in the United States first met at work.[1] Melinda and Bill Gates met at work. They met while working together at Microsoft. Their first encounter was at an event where they were seated next to each other.

Melinda recalls: "He was funnier than I expected him to be." So, what's the problem? Not all workplace relationships will succeed like Bill and Melinda.[2]

A college professor told me: "Last year, I worked at a university. I dated a woman named Lisa for a year or two and it wasn't against the policy because (at the time) we were in different departments, but we still kept it a secret. During that time, I helped her get a promotion, but then we broke up."

Not long after, Lisa was transferred to the same department, and the relationship turned south. "She started to try and make me look bad—she spread rumors about my background and expertise. Luckily, she was transferred to another department, but the situation could have made my professional life a nightmare," he said.

Jumping into a relationship with a coworker may seem exciting, but sometimes this recipe can result in a toxic mess that can result in termination—and even worse if it ends up in the courts. To protect themselves, as a result of cases like McDonald's chief executive officer Stephen Easterbrook, Intel's chief executive officer Brian Krzanich, and Uber founder Travis Kalanick[3] (outlined in Chapter 2), companies are rewriting the rules for what is and is not acceptable in the twenty-first century.

> Jumping into a relationship with a coworker may seem exciting, but sometimes this recipe can result in a toxic mess that can result in termination—and even worse if it ends up in the courts.

Relationships between men and women have shifted dramatically in the workplace, but here's something that has remained constant: romance. Human beings come hardwired to gossip, spread rumors, and pass along the latest titillating scandal. When a man and a woman become engaged in a close relationship at work, eyebrows raise, jealousy blossoms, and idle minds begin to race.

Douglas, an executive at a hedge fund that employs seven hundred people, told me that human resources consultants advised the company to implement policies against personal relations between those in authority (supervisors) and direct subordinates. This was a defensive measure taken to protect the company from harassment lawsuits and to raise awareness of the possible pitfalls of workplace relationships.

A woman who is a manager at a federal government organization in Washington, DC, told me: "The point about work and relationships is that if a supervisor is dating a direct report then it affects the morale of the whole team. It's okay for employees to date each other, but not a boss and subordinate." This kind of relationship is unacceptable because it can impact other employees' morale. Are they receiving preferential treatment because they are dating the boss? Did they get a raise or a promotion because they're sleeping with the manager?

> "The point about work and relationships is that if a supervisor is dating a direct report then it affects the morale of the whole team. It's okay for employees to date each other, but not a boss and subordinate."

David Drummond, the chief legal officer at Google, faced accusations of inappropriate relationships with employees. Yet Drummond's relationships were both consensual and with an employee from a different department, not a direct report. Whether or not you agree with the new enforced corporate policies, don't date women at work. It's just not worth it.

According to a survey published by CareerBuilder, following high-profile accusations of sexual harassment, the frequency of office romances has declined. This survey revealed that 36 percent of workers report dating a coworker, down from 40 percent.[4] I imagine this could also be due to the increased popularity of online dating websites and apps like Zoosk, Match, and eHarmony.

The older you are, the more likely you are to seek a relationship in the workplace. Seventy-two percent of workers aged fifty and older reported having at least one romantic workplace relationship during their career.[5] How many of these relationships today are going to end with either marriage or a great friendship? If a workplace fling dissolves like the vast majority of romances, you (as an employee) are left in close proximity to a disgruntled coworker who a) no longer has affection for you, or b) has dirt on you. And that's a problem.

It is important that corporations encourage social connections, but you must be clear about boundaries. Falling in love, or lust, feels great. However, it can create distractions at work and cause productivity to suffer. If you're in a leadership role, be clear about romance in the office. Set a policy that addresses how the company will respond if a relationship like this ensues.

For example, more companies are asking romantically involved coworkers to sign a **Love Contract**. Love Contracts are designed to establish guidelines around workplace dating.[6] Such a contract typically declares that both parties are in a consensual relationship, takes sexual harassment lawsuits off the table, and requires arbitration in the event of a grievance around the relationship.[7] Some companies require managers who date subordinates to disclose that relationship and state that one party in the relationship be reassigned to a different department so there is no "supervisory relationship." **The Bottom Line:** Do your best to separate workplace relationships from personal relationships.

You're Dating Your Coworker. Now What?

Men are known for their ability to strip away emotion to make rational decisions, and workplace relationships are an area where they need that coolheaded reasoning more than ever.

If you ignored my advice above, and you're dating your coworker, you're putting both parties in a tough spot. You could be endangering both of your careers. The best thing to do is encourage transparency and discourage romantic relationships between managers and subordinates. You must follow whatever rules exist and notify the appropriate officials. Be discreet and don't use the relationship in a way that either benefits or disadvantages your coworker at work. Most employers have common policies regarding workplace relationships—know what they are and abide by them. Some of these rules include:

- Mandatory disclosure of the relationship to the human resources department
- A ban on relationships between superiors and subordinates
- The signing of Love Contract agreements and acknowledgment of company anti–sexual harassment policies
- A ban on public displays of affection within the workplace[8]

As you can imagine, some policy requirements, like a "mandatory disclosure," can be a real tripwire. This makes it very easy for management to punish or fire someone without wading into the actual relationship itself. Simply not self-reporting can be a "crime." If you're serious about the relationship, here's a better solution: request that you be transferred to a different department. If each party in the relationship has a different direct report, the relationship *may* be acceptable.

What if you're *not* dating your coworker, but there's a perception that you are? It's all about the optics. Neil was a partner at a transportation company in Memphis, Tennessee, and he told me that he actually had to quit his job because his wife thought he was having an extramarital affair with his young, attractive assistant. At the new firm, Neil refused to hire a young or attractive woman and settled for an elderly man, whom he presumed to be the least risky choice for him. Although the elderly man wasn't the most qualified, Neil's wife approved of his assistant.

Furthermore, companies should discourage any type of personal relationships in the office, not just dating, but family and husband/wife partnerships too. Why? Because performance evaluations, promotions, or bonuses can be seen as biased, even if they're not.

In some instances, like a family office or family business—hiring your spouse may make sense for the company's strategic goals. If that's the case, a company-wide email stating that such relationships are discouraged in the workplace should be enough. This would provide both employers and employees with wiggle room, versus an explicit rule in the company policy handbook.

A policy handbook is actually a corporate contract. Quite often, employees don't even know they have legally agreed to it.[9] A simple acceptance via email may be enough to professionally bind you to this workplace agreement. Employers do not necessarily need an employee's signature when arbitration provisions are included in the manual itself, and a Read Receipt Email Certificate can also be added.[10] So, please, read the policy handbook.

> A policy handbook is actually a corporate contract. Quite often, employees don't even know they have legally agreed to it.

Human Resources Protects the Company, Not You

If you are engaged in a romantic relationship in the office, just remember—your human resources department exists to protect the company, not you. A senior executive of a major cable news network told me, "HR runs the company." Post-#MeToo, many executives have become fearful of reputational damage and lawsuits, and human resources are taking preventive measures to new heights. Human resources departments have issued new policies regarding sexual harassment and mandated sexual harassment training.

Streaming service provider Netflix was rumored to have banned workers from looking at one another "for more than five seconds" and asking for phone numbers. According to a report, "You mustn't ask for someone's number unless they have given permission for it to be distributed. And if you see any unwanted behavior, report it immediately."[11] Whether or not this is true, staring at anyone longer than five seconds can be seen as kinda creepy. As you can imagine, policies like this have sparked sarcasm—employees look at each other, count to five, and then divert their eyes. Employees were also urged not to prolong hugs or ask people out more than once.[12] I would agree that is sound (and obvious) advice.

My friend Michael is a lawyer for the largest law firm in Baltimore. He told me that the industry mandates for all employees to watch a series of anti-harassment videos that are borderline ridiculous. One video featured a woman who complimented a man's tie. In response, the man said he felt "violated." Really?

Sexual harassment trainings can reinforce men's feelings that women are "emotional and duplicitous in the way that they both want sexual attention, but don't want sexual harassment," said Justine Tinkler, assistant professor of sociology at the University of Georgia.[13] Another professor said she suspects the backlash could stem from the "cartoonish, somewhat unrealistic" harassment examples within these trainings.[14]

Sexual harassment courses aimed at preventing workplace discrimination can have the opposite effect—making men less capable of perceiving inappropriate behavior and more likely to blame victims.[15]

> Sexual harassment courses aimed at preventing workplace discrimination can have the opposite effect–making men less capable of perceiving inappropriate behavior and more likely to blame victims.

How? While studies testing the effects of harassment training are limited, some research suggests counterintuitive and troubling consequences—that after men complete these trainings, they may be more inclined to brush aside allegations and discount victims.[16]

These policies might be driven by an individual company, corporate headquarters, or in response to state and municipal requirements. For example, New York City enacted the Stop Sexual Harassment in NYC Act, which requires employers with fifteen or more employees to conduct mandatory annual anti–sexual harassment training. In California, employers with fifty or more employees are required by law to provide at least two hours of harassment prevention training.[17]

If your company is increasing visibility around its sexual harassment policies, you're not alone. Challenger, Gray & Christmas, Inc., a Chicago-based career consulting firm, reported that 52 percent of companies are reviewing their sexual harassment policies, and more than half of those have updated their policies.[18]

Are you nervous about hiring a woman, especially in roles like an executive assistant where it can be such a personal job? I don't blame you. When a man spends more time at work with his assistant than he does with his wife, it becomes a risk-management decision.

I interviewed Eric, vice president of software development at the nation's largest technology employer. The tech company has one of the nation's most highly skilled workforces and had a big agenda to hire women into senior management roles.

Eric is outspoken and gregarious, but he is also a complete gentleman. His assistant, Rebecca, happily worked for him for more than two years. She absolutely adored him and he was her mentor—her ticket to climbing the corporate ladder. Since most of their office time at work was spent coding (and therefore chained to their desks), on Tuesdays Eric treated Rebecca to an early dinner at a nearby restaurant to discuss business. At dinner, they brainstormed ideas and went over new development plans. There was never, ever one issue or behavioral complaint filed against either one.

One day, Eric received a call from the human resources department in New York. The tech company told Eric that a client had seen the two of them at a restaurant together, which was true. They went there every Tuesday.

Eric recalls HR saying: "We are not the moral police. We just want to make sure the sexual relationship is consensual . . . and if so, please put it in writing." But they were both married! And no such thing was going on.

Apparently, per company policy and code of conduct, employees are not allowed to have a "personal relationship" with anyone they work with. And they are not allowed to meet with colleagues to discuss work outside of the office. Can you believe it?

In the twenty-plus years that Eric worked for the company, this came as a complete surprise. Why? He had always treated his prior assistants to dinner and there was never an issue with it. So, what was the difference this time? His current assistant is a woman, whereas his prior assistants were men. In today's corporate culture, there may be a different set of rules for each gender or at least a double standard.

In today's corporate culture, there may be a different set of rules for each gender or at least a double standard.

So, what was the accusation? That Eric was "overly friendly." Not sexual harassment. Not bullying. Not lack of performance. Simply an accusation of being *overly friendly*.

The next morning, he was served. On his desk, he found a hardcopy letter outlining details of the accusations. The human resources department began firing off insinuating questions: "Have you ever paid Rebecca's rent?" "Have you ever slept together?" "Have you ever given her any form of non-cash compensation?" What? No. Absolutely no such thing ever occurred, he told me. Human resources then called the young woman to interview her.

Human resources: "Has Eric ever made you feel uncomfortable?"

Rebecca: "No. You are making me feel uncomfortable."

In Eric's case, the pendulum had swung too far—HR practices like this are intrusive and undercut legitimate privacy. The company was wrong. The actions taken by the human resources department were taken solely to protect the company, not the woman. They were, sadly, just doing their job in today's inclusive corporate culture.

On the subject of creating compliance protocol to defend a company against lawsuits, human resources departments have been wildly successful. But when it comes to solving sexual harassment issues, human resources departments have failed.

> On the subject of creating compliance protocol to defend a company against lawsuits, human resources departments have been wildly successful. But when it comes to solving sexual harassment issues, human resources departments have failed.

Don't Forget This: Human resources departments exist to protect corporations, not you. As you can see from the number of prominent men who have been fired due to sexual harassment allegations, they won't hesitate to sacrifice even a long-term leader if it serves to insulate the company. Your job is to protect yourself, your brand, and your reputation, because no one else will.

Coming Soon: More Anti-Harassment Training

Anaeli Petisco is an employment attorney. Like it or not, she told me that all employers should mandate "ongoing sexual harassment training." Due to the male/female relationship in the workplace, more anti-harassment training is coming soon.

Petisco said, "At a minimum, the company should host a yearly in-person meeting." Moreover, employees should expect language such as "We do not condone sexual harassment at the workplace" in the policy handbook. Today, this goes both ways—male to female and female to male. "Most importantly, the manual should include a chain-of-command for reporting any instances (or perceived instances) of sexual harassment," she told me.

> "Most importantly, the manual should include a chain-of-command for reporting any instances (or perceived instances) of sexual harassment."

This is key for human resources to protect employers and the company. This type of language must be spelled out in the manual because this can be a prime affirmative defense for companies in court.

Don't be surprised if more mandates and training related to preventing sexual harassment descend from the powers above. A *Journal of Applied Behavioral Science* study evaluated a sexual harassment program for university employees.[19] It found that men who participated in the training were "significantly less likely" to consider coercive behavior toward a subordinate as sexual harassment when compared with a control group of men who hadn't done the training.

Some researchers believe such trainings have no positive effects, and tend to be more about legal cover than meaningful prevention or may even have unintended negative consequences—raising serious concerns about the way that companies heavily focus on training as a solution to harassment.[20]

A study published in the *Social Psychology Quarterly* found that after men learned about harassment rules, it triggered implicit gender biases, effectively making it more likely for them to stereotype women.[21] Justine Tinkler, coauthor of this study, said: "The purpose of sexual harassment policy is to make men and women more equal in the workplace, [but] if the policies are sort of activating gender stereotypes rather than challenging them, they may not be promoting that broader goal."

> "The purpose of sexual harassment policy is to make men and women more equal in the workplace, [but] if the policies are sort of activating gender stereotypes rather than challenging them, they may not be promoting that broader goal."

The best way to combat workplace sexual harassment is to reduce gender inequality and promote women in leadership positions. Even if you're in a consensual relationship, perception is everything. If you need further proof that a romantic relationship could threaten your job, refer back to the stories in Chapter 2. It's just not worth it.

The Secret Rules to Successfully Work with Women

Abide by these rules, and you'll be just fine.

With gender lines blurring in the workplace, it's no wonder that rules and expectations are in flux. This creates confusion about how men and women can effectively work together. Recent headlines around sexual harassment put the subject in the spotlight, making harassment seem like the norm—rather than the exception—in today's workplace. In a survey by *GQ* and *Glamour* magazine, 84 percent of men confessed fear that accusations of sexual misconduct could hurt the reputations of men who didn't do anything wrong.[1]

> Eighty-four percent of men confessed fear that accusations of sexual misconduct could hurt the reputations of men who didn't do anything wrong.

Taking this a step further, many men hesitate to collaborate with women in the workplace because they are fearful of unfounded sexual misconduct accusations. According to a joint survey by SurveyMonkey and LeanIn.org, senior-level men are twelve times more likely to be hesitant about a one-on-one meeting with a junior woman than they are a junior man.[2] Why? Out of fear of an out-of-the-blue sexual harassment allegation.[3]

Clearly, if you're fearful of an unjust accusation, you're not alone. Confusion over how workplace rules have changed drives this anxiety, cutting off productive business relationships, and potentially damaging the careers of many hardworking men.

Relax! This chapter offers a comprehensive guide to The Secret Rules of the workplace. Yes, you can still exhibit masculine traits at work in a feminist world. Yes, you can still associate with, mentor, and collaborate with women in the workplace. And, yes, you can take some commonsense steps to protect yourself. These rules will help clue you in on how to act, what to say, and what to do.

The Secret Rules

Secret Rule #1: Keep Communication Professional

Let's get this out of the way immediately—never, ever send a sexually explicit picture to a coworker. If you do, these images may haunt you forever, showing up decades later. It's easy for remarks to be taken out of context in a text message, particularly in the #MeToo era, with more employers and coworkers calling out the kinds of jokes and comments that may have been given a pass in the past.

It's time to ensure your workplace communications are professional. Scan all of your communications before you send them because it's much harder to see nuances in emails and text messages versus handwritten documents. What you might think is funny or sarcastic could be mistakenly construed by someone else as harassment or hostility. In fact, messaging mistakes are more frequently reported to managers than you might think. On Second Thought reported that 5 percent of employees stated that their messaging mistake was reported to a manager.[4] (Refer to Chapter 7 for more tips on communication.)

Follow the same guidelines to govern your emails and conversations. Ask yourself: What impact are these words going to have on your colleague? How could this be interpreted by the recipient? Use these strategies when emailing or texting at work:

- Demonstrate respect for your colleagues in written communications, emails, and messaging at work.
- Read your company's communication policy and follow it.
- Unsure whether a communication is appropriate? When in doubt, don't send it.
- Step away from the keyboard. Don't fire off an email if you haven't thought things through, especially if there is an urgent need to immediately send it.

Secret Rule #2: Respect Personal Space

Hugging, cheek-kissing, and handshaking all involve entering into someone's personal space. While there are many people who prefer not to be touched by people they don't know well, there are other people (like me) who are natural huggers. I love to hug everyone—it's part of my personality, but I understand that many people prefer not to be hugged.

When it comes to touching—shaking hands, a high five, or a fist bump are all okay, according to Jodi Smith, founder of the consulting firm Mannersmith.[5] With other types of touching, Smith said that keeping it light, such as a quick pat on the back or tap on the arm, makes sense. However, touching someone in a prolonged way can lead to trouble, so it's better to steer clear of that type of contact.

As far as hugging goes, there is no real set rule. But please be careful! If you hug your assistant or a female intern that is your subordinate, that person may feel that she can't say no even if she doesn't want to be touched. A brief upper-body hug to a colleague you've worked with for years may be completely acceptable in the workplace, but a full-body hug is not. Consider the context and the industry. **The Bottom Line:** If you're not sure whether it's okay to hug or touch someone, don't. Wave.

Secret Rule #3: Eat Out in Groups

If you feel uncomfortable having a work dinner alone with a woman, don't. Senior-level men are six times more likely to be hesitant to have a work dinner with a junior woman than a junior man.[6]

> Senior-level men are six times more likely to be hesitant to have a work dinner with a junior woman than a junior man.

If you feel this way, you're definitely not alone.

Women have more active brains than men.[7] According to the World Economic Forum, women tend to be stronger than men in empathy, collaboration, self-control, and showing appropriate concern. As we discussed in Chapter 5, capitalize on a woman's collaborative strength by hosting group dinners.

However, if it's a work-related necessity to eat solo with a woman, you don't have to shy away. If you're polite, considerate, and professional, you have nothing to fear in a one-on-one dinner or lunch. For more helpful tips, see Chapter 5.

Secret Rule #4: Give Neutral Compliments

Compliments are a positive way to build workplace rapport. However, they have become somewhat of a land mine in today's inclusive workplace. Complimenting someone on their personal appearance or outfit could be taken the wrong way—depending on the compliment, who is giving it, and who is receiving it. Keep compliments as neutral as possible. For example, "You're very creative," or "Thank goodness I hired someone who is tech-savvy," versus something too personal and suggestive.

As we discussed in Chapter 7, to totally be on the safe side, restrict your compliments to matters related to work. Think about a work-related accolade to offer a colleague such as, "You really handled all the tough questions well during the presentation last week," or "The suggestion you made at the meeting today was right on target." In fact, to support your colleagues in a positive way, making an effort to praise them on a regular basis for work-related achievements will help create a more positive corporate culture.

Secret Rule #5: Make Proper Introductions

When making introductions, the name of the person with the higher position is said first, regardless of gender. For example: "Mrs. Chairman, I'd like you to meet Mr. Employee." However, if the man and woman are equal in terms of title or position, always make the woman the most important person.

> When making introductions, the name of the person with the higher position is said first, regardless of gender.

If you don't know which coworker is "more important," don't drive yourself crazy. You can mention first the name of the person that you would like to flatter. And to encourage the conversation further, you can add some details about the person in the introduction, like where he or she works: "Emily Miller, this is Daniel Rodriguez. Daniel just joined the team as a new client services rep. Emily is the national sales manager."

Occasionally, you may be the new employee in the room, and you may need to introduce yourself. Plan and practice this at home. For example: "Hi. I'm Jamal, vice president of operations for the research and development department. It's a pleasure to meet you all." And, most important, greet everyone in the workplace the same. As we discussed in Chapter 6, the best way to start your day is by saying a simple "Good morning" to everyone.

Secret Rule #6: Keep the Door Open during Meetings

If you're having one-on-one meetings with women in the office, keep the door open, or ask human resources to replace your office door with a transparent glass panel. Trust me, HR will do anything it can to protect the company or mitigate liabilities. A survey conducted by *Hollywood Reporter* and Morning Consult revealed that 55 percent of men surveyed are fearful of women making false sexual harassment and assault claims at work.[8]

> Fifty-five percent of men surveyed are fearful of women making false sexual harassment and assault claims at work.

I understand why you're concerned; especially after so many reports of sexual harassment cases in the media, it's wise to be cautious. That being said, there are times when you will need to meet in private with female subordinates to provide highly personal feedback or a personnel review. In that case, I reiterate—as long as you behave with consideration and professionalism, you won't risk an unfounded accusation.

Secret Rule #7: Think Before You Speak

Whether you're speaking in front of your colleagues formally or during informal, day-to-day conversations, remember to think before you speak. Never be afraid to hesitate and pull your thoughts together before you talk. In fact, pausing before you say something you might regret shows that you have common sense and self-control. Follow the THINK acronym before you speak: Is what you are going to say **T**houghtful, **H**onest, **I**ntelligent, **N**ecessary, or **K**ind? If not, don't say it.

One of the biggest ways to run afoul of today's secret workplace rules is to engage in locker room talk with male colleagues. Conversing like this in the office is not something you can easily dismiss if you're overheard. It's flat-out offensive, not just to the person you're talking about, but to the people you're talking to. It can make other men uncomfortable if they don't agree with what you're saying. There is no place in the workplace for this kind of talk. Staying away from it is one of the best ways you can protect yourself from an accusation of harassment.

Secret Rule #8: Dress for Success

A few years ago, it was easy to tell who was a professional and who wasn't. Why? Because all businessmen wore suits. Today, it seems like anything goes when it comes to dress at work, even in conservative occupations such as a corporate lawyer or an investment banker. As we will discuss in Chapter 13, I believe that this cultural change is unleashing confusion about what it means to be a professional. Research from staffing firm OfficeTeam suggests that your clothing choices affect how you are perceived by others, as well as your chances of being promoted in your job.[9]

> Your clothing choices affect how you are perceived by others, as well as your chances of being promoted in your job.

Wearing a suit to work establishes your level of professionalism. If your occupation requires a uniform or you can dress casually in the office, lucky you! **Just Remember:** Acting and dressing like a professional businessman sends signals to your colleagues that you take your job seriously.

Secret Rule #9: Hold the Door for Everyone

Just like smiling and greeting, opening the door and holding it open is a friendly, positive gesture. It's the right thing to do. I hold the door for everyone. Of course, a woman is more than capable of doing this on her own, but it's the awareness of someone's presence that shows true consideration. A female sales executive at a Fortune 500 pharmaceutical company told me, "I want a man to open the door for me, but I'm not going to get his coffee." Contrary to popular belief, most women welcome this kind of gesture.

If a woman starts opening the door for herself, just pull it open further. There's no need to knock her hand off the door handle or offer any sanctimonious "I insist" or "Allow me" entreaties. **The Bottom Line:** Don't make a big deal about it.

And female employees aren't your only concern when it comes to opening doors. Opening a door for a supervisor is a sign of respect. When you're entering a building with your boss, it's customary for you to open the door for your boss and then follow behind.

Secret Rule #10: Give a Consistent Handshake

Post-coronavirus, we live in a new normal, including frequent handwashing. If you or a colleague may be sick, an "elbow bump" may be acceptable. A realtor based in Bethesda, Maryland, regularly shook hands as often as possible. But, during COVID-19, he had to "fight the deeply ingrained instinct to extend his hand."[10] If you're a hypochondriac, keep a small bottle of hand sanitizer in your pocket. Why? Because handshakes are often seen as a vital part of a job interview and a way to respectfully greet coworkers in a formal office setting.

"I don't think we should ever shake hands again."

–Dr. Anthony Fauci

In most corporate industries, everyone is still expected to shake hands during the initial encounter. In fact, it's a good idea to keep your right hand free. Before you walk into a meeting, move anything you are carrying to your left hand. Dr. Melissa Garretson, a pediatric emergency physician in Texas, was flabbergasted when a male colleague asked her if it was okay to shake hands anymore.[11] She replied, "Are you kidding me?" It's important not to overreact for fear of being accused of sexual harassment.

If you're not sure whether you should change the way you shake hands when you are greeting a woman, quit wondering. Maintain a consistent handshake, not softening or tightening based on whether you're shaking hands with a man or a woman.

Secret Rule #11: Listen Actively

When a woman speaks with you, she is talking because she wants to be heard. She doesn't necessarily want you to agree with her and (most likely) isn't looking for your advice. As we discussed in Chapter 8, active listening refers to a pattern of listening that keeps you engaged with your coworker in a positive way. It is the process of listening attentively while a colleague is speaking, paraphrasing and reflecting back on what is said, and most important, withholding any judgment or advice.

When you do this, you make the other person feel both understood and valued. It's the foundation for any successful conversation. Pretend you are a therapist listening to a client; you are there to be a sounding board rather than ready to interrupt with your own opinions and solutions about what is being said.

Active listening differs from critical listening in that you are not evaluating the message of the person with the goal of finding a solution; rather, the goal is simply for the other person to be heard. As a supervisor, this will allow you to understand problems at work and collaborate with your female partners to develop solutions. It also reflects patience, which is a valuable quality in any job.

> Active listening differs from critical listening in that you are not evaluating the message of the person with the goal of finding a solution; rather, the goal is simply for the other person to be heard.

Secret Rule #12: Treat Everyone with Respect

What some may call chivalry, I call respect. Some may say that chivalry is somehow demeaning or discriminatory against women, but this is not the majority. Chivalry is still appreciated. Regardless of whether women say it out loud or not, they still want to be treated nicely, with attention and respect. **The Bottom Line:** Treat everyone like a human being. The Golden Rule is always applicable—treat others the way you would like to be treated.

A corporate culture of respect and self-worth thrives when employees feel their efforts get noticed. At the heart of a successful company is a culture of mutual respect that starts from the top and trickles down to the cleaning crew. Studies show employees are 26 percent more likely to leave their jobs if they feel there is a lack of respect among colleagues. So, how do you prevent this? Engage in purposeful communication (see Chapter 7), avoid negative criticism (use constructive feedback), and put a stop to negativity.

Secret Rule #13: Find Commonalities

A great salesperson knows what the other person is thinking. Salespeople understand and communicate on the prospect's terms because that's the only way you'll be able to lead the prospect to arrive at your solution. Even if you're not in sales—discovering commonalities with female colleagues is your key to better relationships with them.

This can be as simple as inquiring about where a new employee or coworker lives or went to school. Remember the "Art of Small Talk" outlined in Chapter 5? If you're married or have children, and you know the other person does, too, then talk about them.

Before you meet with someone, an easy way to find commonalities and show you care is to check out their background on the company website or on a business networking site such as LinkedIn. Breaking the ice with new employees or a new boss is so much easier when they know you've already taken the initiative to learn something about them. It makes them feel important. Once you find more points of commonality than differences, you're more likely to view others favorably, and in turn, they're also more likely to have a favorable impression of you.

> Once you find more points of commonality than differences, you're more
> likely to view others favorably, and in turn, they're also more likely to have a
> favorable impression of you.

The Seven Deadly Sins on the Job

What not to do at the office.

For the 99.9 percent of men who want to be part of the solution, or at least not be part of the problem, it can be a confusing world. Many men now feel they're guilty until proven innocent, and not just when it comes to HR. While, yes, there are creeps out there, I'm going to assume you're not one of them (or you wouldn't be reading this book).

Do you fear that you may have offended a female coworker without even knowing it? Many men don't know how to behave at work in the twenty-first century. That's not a cop-out, it's just a fact. Women are entering the workforce in droves, and this has changed the dynamic completely. There are plenty of books telling women how to behave and what to do to be successful. But for men, it's different. You now work in a world that is fraught with gender politics and conflicting points of view. I often hear the following: "I don't know when a female employee is going to take offense." "I don't know where the line is between funny and insensitive." Or, "What do my female coworkers really want?"

The answer is simple. They want what you want. They want the chance to build a successful career and accomplish their goals. They want to be able to go to work and not worry that their ideas are going to be shot down, or that they're going to be spoken over, or treated as an outsider.

Here's a story (gone wrong) of a company that set out to make an example—justly or unjustly—simply to show the industry that they were avid about protecting women. My friend Benjamin (Ben) works at the second largest accounting firm in the country. He received an outrageous and totally specious "Written Warning" letter from the human resources department regarding personal Instant Messages with two of his employees:

> This memorandum shall serve as a written warning that your recent behavior and conduct are below the standards the firm expects. We understand that you deny being involved in a personal relationship with your employees, and our review did not conclude otherwise. However, the Instant Message communications between you and both of these employees reflect a flirtatious tone initiated by you that's against our policy rules.

The letter goes on to say:

> You reflected poor judgment . . . including commenting on their appearance and clothing. Employees are expected to perform their job responsibilities satisfactorily and adhere to the Code of Conduct.
>
> We also want to take this opportunity to remind you that per the Firm's Personal Relationships Policy, you are required to report the existence of any personal relationship to a member of management and/or the human resources department. Failure to provide prompt notification may result in termination.
>
> As a result of this investigation, we are requiring you to participate in an online training course called "Employee Fairness." This Written Warning will be assessed as part of your annual conduct review and may impact your eligibility for promotion and impact future compensation.

Really? It's important to note that no complaint had ever been expressed or filed. Ben had never, ever received any type of notice or warning in the past, and neither employee felt that their boss was being "flirtatious." Even HR's own investigation revealed that their accusations were unfounded.

Here was Ben's response:

> I have not pursued a personal intimate relationship with any coworker. These accusations are unfounded, no policy violations were actually identified, and I have no prior history of any behavioral concerns. You said I broke the rule, but I don't know what the rule is.

That's the problem! Companies don't define the rules, so they can punish at will. The response continued . . .

> The conclusion reached by HR agreed that no such personal relationships had ever taken place. In fact, the two women who were accused of engaging in personal intimate relationships with me confirmed that no such relationships ever occurred, and they emphatically stated that I did not act unprofessionally or inappropriately toward them or ever make them feel uncomfortable for any reason.

The Bottom Line: Companies are doing two things—protecting the brand and setting an example. Shoot now, ask questions later. The Secret Rules in Chapter 10 told you what to do. Here are "seven deadly sins" to help you know what *not* to do.

#1 Not Thinking before You Speak

Words have power, including the power to change things. Chris, a customer service representative at an airline company in Fort Worth, Texas, told me the following story: A flight attendant hobbled into a meeting in the office. She had just flown in from another office. She was lugging a couple of large travel bags with her stuff and pushed them against the wall, but Chris didn't see her carrying them in.

At some point during the meeting, her bags tipped over and made a loud noise, interrupting the conversation. Chris quickly apologized for not helping her store the bags properly in the back room. He said if he ever saw another woman walk in with bags that he would "scramble to help her out." The woman was offended. She thought, *I don't need any help just because I'm a woman. Is he implying I am not physically strong enough to carry them myself?*

Chris explained to me that he sincerely said this out of kind consideration for his colleague, but later realized that he should not have referenced gender. When in doubt, ask yourself: *Would I act the same way or say the same thing to a male colleague?*

#2 Inappropriate Touching

Both the #MeToo movement and the coronavirus pandemic have accelerated a workplace culture of no touching—forming a negative association with any kind of social touch. However, inappropriate touching still happens. A manager once grabbed me by my belt and pulled me toward him—not in a sexual nature, but more as a command to move in closer to the employee group chat. This was inappropriate.

The manager was the head honcho at the gym. And it wasn't just any gym—it was an international fitness chain that pioneered the industry. As a general manager in a place where women show their rear ends and men are fired up on caffeine and creatine powder, this was no place for the politically correct. I didn't take it personally, and I never filed a complaint, but it just felt uncomfortable. Boundaries are important in today's inclusive corporate culture.

#3 Bullying

Perhaps the biggest threat to a company's bottom line are bad bosses. Your day-to-day relationship with your direct supervisor is directly correlated to your overall well-being at the company.

In a previous job, my boss bullied me. After one meeting, he shoved me against a brick wall outside and accused me of misstating a minor data point. He disparaged and insulted me frequently, to the point where I would go home in tears almost every day. It wasn't exactly what he said, it was *how* he said things. I realized that his behavior wasn't going to change and that I couldn't tolerate it. Despite having been at that company for nearly a decade, I decided to quit. He was fired about one year later.

If you're on the receiving end of being bullied—never hesitate to report any form of bullying to your boss, a trusted colleague, or the human resources department. That was my biggest mistake. I didn't tell anyone. Don't submit to constant badgering or criticism that you feel is unfair. Speak up!

#4 Making Inappropriate Jokes

There are a number of cases that focus on offhand comments made in the workplace. These comments often come back later as evidence of discriminatory intent or harassment. Almost all harassers claim that they were "just joking." And often the comments were intended to just be *jokes*. Unfortunately, a jury doesn't laugh when the case is decided.

Sometimes the court rules that the comments were not sufficiently severe to establish a case. However, a company still has to waste time and money to defend something that could have been avoided altogether; this is known as a Pyrrhic victory (as we discuss in Chapter 12). In other words, the company may win the battle, but in the process, it lost a great deal.

Remember the CEO in Chapter 7 who told a joke about Alex Rodriguez during a conference, which some women deemed to be sexist? As we discussed in "The Humor Advantage," jokes have their place, but not in the workplace. People have feelings and jokes can be taken the wrong way. Making people laugh is a great way to get them to like you, but in an increasingly politically correct culture, you have to be careful about the kinds of jokes you tell. Stick to safe subjects—like sports, music, or entertainment. And never, ever trash-talk your company or its policies. That will get you fired.

#5 Disrespecting Privacy

Not only are jokes one of the worst offenders of interoffice relationships; there are ergonomic factors also, or physical barriers and situations. One example is the area or space better known as a cubicle. Don't you just love cubicles? Like organic eggs, you're not quite caged, but you're not quite free-range either. Or maybe your company has no walls and you sit in a big open area, with absolutely no privacy.

In a past financial sales job, I sat in a cubicle all day making sales calls to prospective clients. My manager, Tim, sat in the cubicle right behind me—looking and lurching. Just knowing he was in there, separated by something as thin as a pasteboard box just tormented me. He was too close for comfort and made himself known at the drop of a hat. For example, if my phone rang, he would bolt upright out of his seat to spy.

Every day I finished my required number of calls and exceeded my daily tasks much faster than anyone else in the office. As soon as I was done, Tim popped his head over my cubicle and became a Roman statue (as if I didn't know he was creepily standing there the entire time).

I always felt like I was under a microscope. It was very weird, like office stalking. To this day, I still can't figure out what he was doing—was he bored? Or just fascinated by how quickly I got my work done? Nonetheless, Tim's behavior led to several formal complaints to his manager and a formal request to be moved to a different location in the office, which never happened.

The Bottom Line: Don't stand over someone else's cubicle. It looks like you're eavesdropping. Try to focus on your own work projects, not your employee's projects. Respect the privacy of others, even if you are banished to cubicle life. Instead of making a beeline for your colleague's cubicle, get in touch in advance. Ask when it might be a convenient time to stop by. And then, when you get there, knock before you enter their personal space. Yes, knock. Ask if it's a good time to talk.

#6 Excessive Drinking at Happy Hour

Many men have battened down the hatches at work. In the flash of a news cycle, a request for drinks after work could be turned into a hit piece. Here's one of them:

> The bar cut off the music. We went twenty minutes over our karaoke room's reservation. My boss, totally drunk, started rapping into the microphone about everyone on our team at work. A karaoke bar employee chased him around for several minutes, trying to wrestle the mic from him while he continued his freestyle rap cataloging everybody's role on the team.

How embarrassing! This may surprise you, but happy hour with coworkers is still a business function. It's not a social function. Ever. I repeat: happy hour is not an invitation to party with the office. No matter how relaxed the atmosphere is, your coworkers are still watching. Your boss is still watching. You can easily say or do something you regret if you are inebriated. Here are some tips to avoid getting tipsy:

- Order a nonalcoholic beverage (request a slice of lime on the side and no one will know).
- Order a drink you don't like and nurse it all evening (like a whiskey sour?).
- Set a limit for yourself (how about two?).
- Set a prearranged limit with the bartender ahead of time (they will thank you later).

How you conduct yourself at so-called social events (work) is just as important as your behavior at the office. Keep in mind, your supervisor may be testing you during these "social" outings. Drink when you get home, when you're alone, or when you're with your nonjudgmental friends from college or high school who similarly want to cut loose. So, if you act stupid, no one will judge you. Is it really worth sabotaging your potential promotion?

#7 Using Terms of Endearment

A Bank of America employee who worked as a relationship manager at the company sued after saying she was subjected to discrimination. In a complaint filed in federal court, she said that clients used vulgar language, calling her "sweetie" and "honey."[1] *That's "vulgar" language?*

Southerners often use terms like "sweetie" and "honey." People who work in New York City or Beverly Hills may find it common to address others as "babe." Europeans working in the United States may greet coworkers with one expressive kiss on the check, or even two. However, these types of affection and terms of endearment in the workplace could now be perceived as unacceptable behavior and even get you written up. (*I know, these are crazy times we live in.*)

What is acceptable to a woman in one place may not be acceptable in another. Calling a client "darling" might go over better in Boston than in Atlanta. The easiest way to remember this is to ask yourself if you would use the same term to address a male coworker. If the answer is no, then find another endearing term. People have names. Use them.

"A person's name is to that person, the sweetest, most important sound in any language."[2]
—Dale Carnegie

Remembering the names of your colleagues is critical to your ongoing professional success. It is essential in forming and strengthening relationships with others, as well as establishing rapport with your coworkers. If you're not good at remembering names, either take notes immediately after the meeting, or ask a colleague to help you.

In other words, learn the appropriate social and business "code of conduct" and adhere to it. Business greetings have their place and their importance in communications. Just think before you speak and use the same endearing terms that you would use toward a male coworker. Then you'll be safe. This doesn't mean that you can never use an endearing term; you simply must pay attention to when, where, and to whom you use it. **The Bottom Line:** Professional communication is always best.

How to Protect Yourself

Don't make dumb mistakes. Know what they are and how to avoid them.

"A woman can say one thing about you and then your life is gone."
—Steve Carell, *The Morning Show*

Apple TV's *The Morning Show* is a portrait of male defensiveness and denial in the wake of #MeToo. Here's the truth: the vast majority of women today aren't interested in taking you down or giving you grief.

Let me repeat: The vast majority of women today aren't interested in taking you down or giving you grief. But the truth is, *some are.* Our powerful female rights don't give us the right to unjustly disrespect you either. Surprise! Women don't have the right to belittle, disparage, libel, or slander you, or make your life a living hell in the workplace. And honestly, this type of behavior is bad for women everywhere. When a woman is unjustly pointing fingers, she makes it harder for women with legitimate complaints.

If you expect all women to be fair-minded about accusations of harassment in the workplace, then you have misjudged the trajectory of

#MeToo's world orbit. Due process and presumed innocence are not always part of the equation. Instead, the default belief is to accept the "victim's" story.

There are new rules, regulations, and workplace protocols that apply to both genders. But with this new emphasis on supporting workplace gender equality comes the opportunity for abuse—for non-victims to convince themselves or others that they suffer at your misogynistic hands, and that turnabout is somehow fair play.

Don't Ruffle Feathers

Have you ever watched the movie *Animal House*? The frat boys are on trial when their spokesman, Eric Stratton, launches into their defense. Stratton's defense is one of Hollywood's most well-known scenes and shows how trying to brush off youthful indiscretions with "everybody does it" simply won't fly anymore in today's inclusive corporate culture.

In today's #MeToo culture, employers from all corporate industries—from aerospace, technology, and fast-food companies to internet service providers and politicians—are reacting to sexual harassment claims (or even consensual workplace relationships) with a super-sensitivity that comes from fear of liability. Even a throwaway comment regarding sexual innuendo or flirting in the workplace now typically leads to a chain of "cover your butt" procedures: consult the lawyer, mandate sensitivity training for everyone, interview the parties to the (non)event, instruct and reinstruct everyone about the perils of such conduct—whether it happened or not.

In a small-business setting, taking these remedial measures basically confirms the worst in everyone's minds—we wouldn't be getting this type of training if some sort of misconduct didn't happen. It's often the ultimate "guilt first, evidence later" approach to harassment accusations. Sometimes the employer reaction is even more extreme—sanctioning or suspending employees, with or without any shred of due process; searching emails and texts for evidence of inappropriate communication; and quietly derailing dreams of advancement because a star chamber, operating in secrecy, has decided that you now "bring baggage" to the firm.

A Little Advice

Men only count for one in five workplace sexual harassment complaints. But a CNBC survey revealed that only 10 percent of men actually report sexual harassment or misconduct at work.[1] Of course, just because it's not reported doesn't mean it isn't happening.

| Men only count for one in five workplace sexual harassment complaints.

If a man belittles a woman, it's harassment. If a woman belittles a man, nobody cares. Yes, this is called a double standard. Certain things like quid pro quo harassment—grabbing a coworker's butt, exposing oneself to another employee, or telling an employee that she will get a promotion if she sleeps with you—are clear-cut cases of sexual harassment. But there are broader categories of harassment that may not have even dawned on you as a problem. There are instances and categories of unacceptable behavior you've never dreamed of that could be grounds for termination. Remember what happened to the CEOs in Chapter 1?

Reputation-management consultant Temin and Company reported more than 810 high-profile figures who have recently been accused of improper sexual conduct.[2] These include McDonald's chief executive officer Stephen Easterbrook, Google executive Andy Rubin, Wynn Resorts founder Steve Wynn, Sherpa Capital founder Shervin Pishevar, Intel's chief executive officer Brian Krzanich, Binary Capital cofounder Justin Caldbeck, and Uber founder Travis Kalanick.[3] But, you may ask, what if the claims aren't true? The damage to both you and the company's reputation can still be significant.

In many of the cases noted above, there were multiple accusations of improper sexual conduct and/or sexual harassment. Even if sexual comments or behaviors are inappropriate for the workplace—and result in workplace discipline or dismissal—not everything rises to the level of illegal harassment under the law. Such behavior must create a hostile workplace to be actionable or directly involve demands for sexual favors.

Sexual Harassment Cases Rarely Succeed in Court

A random sampling of sexual harassment cases reveals that half settle out of court, 37 percent are dismissed before trial, and only 2 percent of plaintiffs win their cases at trial.[4] This might come as a surprise, but the odds of a sexual harassment complaint advancing to a court case are quite small because the standard to prove harassment is high.[5] Courts have previously ruled that the alleged harasser must have acted intentionally and that the behavior must have been repeated multiple times to be deemed pervasive.[6] But this doesn't mean that companies won't take action against an employee (guilty or not) due to an alleged allegation to protect their brand and their reputation.

> A random sampling of sexual harassment cases reveals that half settle out of court, 37 percent are dismissed before trial, and only 2 percent of plaintiffs win their cases at trial.

Laura Beth Nielsen, a research professor at the American Bar Foundation and Northwestern University, reports that a single complaint is unlikely to materially affect your job. Multiple complaints could very well cause you to receive some form of discipline from your employer or dismissal from your job. However, while you may be in the clear from the legal perspective, you might suffer irreparable damage to your reputation.

Even if you don't think it's important to protect yourself (because you're not doing anything wrong), *it is*! It's very important to protect yourself. It's like the mandatory bathroom sign, "All Employees Must Wash Their Hands." Post-pandemic, that seems obvious, but it must be said to protect your employer as well as your reputation. Words have power. Accusers are not always right, but sadly, your reputation hinges on something as simple as the words, "He did this . . ." Whether it's true or not. It's all about how your behavior is viewed. It's all about perception.

Regardless of the thoughts you may or may not have in your head, it's how you are perceived that matters—the optics of the situation. Especially with sexual harassment and sexual assault allegations running rampant in the news—any gossip, rumors, or innuendo about your behavior toward women in the workplace spells trouble for you and your employer. And that's a problem. It's wise to avoid even the appearance of impropriety. It may not be fair, but that's the world we live in today.

The best way to protect yourself is to behave in a manner that is completely above reproach. No sexual jokes, no compliments about your assistant's physical appearance, no flirting with colleagues via text, and no asking your female coworker if she has a hot date tonight. In Chapter 2, we learned that McDonald's chief executive officer and Alphabet's (Google's) legal executive were both fired due to consensual relationships. Even a consensual workplace relationship isn't safe anymore. It's just not worth it. Here's proof . . .

Pyrrhic Victories

Court can be a Roman circus. "It's who you know and who you blow." This tasteless comment from one employee to another got the employee fired. Was it a lawful termination? According to the verdict in *Scheidler v. Indiana*, it was.[7] And after six painful years of court battles, it didn't really matter. With the enormous waste of time and money that both sides suffered by then, only one group profited—the lawyers. But this does pose an interesting question: What are the limits of what employees can say to one another? Was the remark by Brenda Lear Scheidler really a complaint about favoritism in the workplace—a "protected activity" for which she should not have been fired?

A **Pyrrhic victory** is a victory that inflicts such a devastating toll on the victor that it is tantamount to defeat.

A Pyrrhic victory is a victory that inflicts such a devastating toll on the victor that it is tantamount to defeat. An employer or employee who wins a Pyrrhic victory has also suffered a heavy toll that negates any true sense of achievement.

The *Scheidler* parties actually debated the meaning of the word *blow*. **Please Hear This:** You do not want to find yourself in a court of law debating the meaning of the word *blow*. The time, effort, and money are not worth it. It's important to make risk-management decisions when faced with difficult employees. Art Bourque, an employment lawyer in Phoenix, has some advice.[8] Here's what a manager can do:

- As a manager, first you must identify the risk.

- Keep a record of times that you have disciplined the employee via email, showing a history of negative performance reviews. If the employee has recently reported misconduct or harassment, then your risk of a retaliation claim and the liability for the company are much higher.

- Be patient. If you want to terminate an employee, but the immediate risk is too high, it is best to wait and establish a better record of discipline for a future termination.

- Document discipline. Write it down.

You do not have control in the courtroom. But you do have control in the workplace. If you've got to watch what you say, so be it. It may not be fun—changing habits is rarely fun or easy. However, after a certain period (conventional wisdom says it takes twenty-one days to break a habit), what previously seemed difficult will become the new normal. Appropriate behavior keeps you and your company on the right side of the law and keeps you out of trouble.

Playing the
Corporate Gentleman Part

How to dress and act like a corporate gentleman.

I t can be quite difficult to make a good impression and deliver the proper image in the modern workplace. What you wear is just as important as what you say and how you say it. And if you're new to the office, first impressions are everything.

A Man's Corporate Style

The truth is: people judge other people based on their appearance. According to *Forbes*: "A first impression at work is made within the first seven seconds of meeting someone and research suggests that a tenth of a second is all it takes to start determining traits like trustworthiness."[1]

> "A first impression at work is made within the first seven seconds of meeting someone and research suggests that a tenth of a second is all it takes to start determining traits like trustworthiness."

Someone's impression of you is made very quickly. Therefore, you must pay attention to the importance of dressing professionally. Your clothes can communicate volumes about you at work: What are you communicating intentionally or unintentionally through your style choices?

An investment bank published a forty-four-page dress code that went viral. The obsessive stipulations detailed everything from the sensible— "If you wear a watch, it suggests reliability and that punctuality is of great concern to you"—to the downright invasive: employees were instructed how to shower and apply lotion, how to wear their underwear, and were told not to eat garlic during the week. I'm not kidding! In the bank's defense, due to enormous pushback, the code was scrapped and executives said, "We are reviewing what's important to us."[2]

Wait! How you dress *is* important.

Due to COVID-19, more people were working from home than ever. An IBM Institute for Business Value survey found more than 75 percent of respondents favored continuing to work remotely post-pandemic. Videoconferences, like Zoom, have become the lifeblood of businesses, and pants are suddenly less important. When a webcam only captures a user's head and upper torso, employees are buying more professional shirts, according to Walmart, but not pants.[3] This is the new norm.

A survey conducted by the recruitment firm Randstad USA revealed that casual dress appears to be the norm in most workplaces. Surprisingly, 33 percent of respondents said they would quit or turn down a job offer if they were required to follow a conservative dress code. Wow! Other key findings include:

- A combined 79 percent of workers report their current employer has a dress code policy that is either business casual, casual, or nonexistent/no dress code at all.

- Sixty-three percent of workers ages eighteen to thirty-five say they prefer dressing up for work because it makes them feel confident, while only 51 percent of older workers agree. Still a majority.

- Seventy-four percent of men surveyed own a suit, compared to 45 percent of women.[4]

Once upon a time, it was a secret rule that men wear suits and ties to work without exception, and women wear dresses and skirts. Then came "Casual Friday," a trend that began in the 1990s in which some businesses relaxed their dress code on Fridays. It goes like this: from Monday to Thursday, employees dress professionally in the workplace, and on Fridays—jeans and a polo. And why not?

Facebook's chief executive officer, Mark Zuckerberg, wears the same T-shirt to work every day. But since you're not Zuckerberg yet, you should at least still wear a shirt with a collar. When asked why he wears T-shirts, Zuckerberg said he wants to limit the time he spends making "frivolous" decisions.[5] But your corporate attire and style are not *frivolous*.

Unfortunately, all these years later, Casual Friday became the everyday norm. Investment bank Goldman Sachs was subject to a strict dress code until recently. The code stipulated that investment bankers must dress elegantly at all times. David Solomon, Goldman Sachs's chief executive officer, sought to change that by getting rid of the dress code. But some experts believe that this decision was completely wrong.

In "Does Wall Street say goodbye to his tie?" *Forbes* interviewed me about this topic: "The new dress code is a bad idea. A suit and a tie are a uniform and make it much easier for minorities and people from other countries to feel comfortable in the workplace," I said. "If investment banks want to open up to new talent and, therefore, to greater diversity, they should keep the suit and tie."[6]

"The new dress code is a bad idea. A suit and a tie are a uniform and make it much easier for minorities and people from other countries to feel comfortable in the workplace."

However, Solomon was not the pioneer of the corporate "no dress code" policy. Silicon Valley tech titans Google, Facebook, and Twitter all allow you to show up to work in just about anything. Although the tech industry's daily responsibilities do not involve meeting with high-net-worth clients, women may feel more comfortable working with you if you're not lounging around the office in flip-flops and pajamas.

The Skirt Length Theory

"You wana get ahead climbing on the shoulders of men, Phyllis, fine.
Just know they're looking right up your skirt."
—Jill Ruckelshaus (Elizabeth Banks), *Mrs. America*

What if I told you that the way women dress at work can actually influence the economy? It's true! **The Skirt Length Theory** is the idea that skirt lengths are a predictor of stock market direction. According to the theory, if short skirts are growing in popularity, it means the stock market is going to go up. Shorter skirts appear in times when consumer confidence is high and the economy is booming. However, if longer skirt lengths are gaining traction in the fashion industry, it may mean that the stock market is about to crash. Economists have observed this phenomenon for a long time.

The Skirt Length Theory was first suggested by Professor George Taylor at the Wharton School of Business in 1925. For example, hemlines were shorter in the 1990s when the tech bubble was increasing, and miniskirts were popular in the 1980s alongside Reagan's economic boom. It was also accurate in 1987, when designers switched from miniskirts to floor-length skirts just before the market crashed.[7]

Isn't that interesting? As the economy grows, the skirts may become shorter, and there is nothing you can say or do about it. Just focus on growing your stock portfolio, because the one thing you definitely don't want to get caught doing in a short-skirt economy is staring at your co-worker's rising hemline. No ogling allowed!

Underwear and Haircuts

Here's another one: **The Men's Underwear Index** (long favored by former Federal Reserve Chairman Alan Greenspan) is an unconventional economic indicator that predicts how well the economy is doing based on men's underwear sales. It suggests that a decline in the sales of men's underwear indicates an overall poor state of the economy, while an increase in purchases predicts an improving economy.[8]

Paul Mitchell founder and stylist John Paul DeJoria sees it a bit differently. He suggests that an increase in the employment data corresponds to men getting a haircut once every six weeks. An increase in the unemployment data corresponds to the frequency of men's haircuts dropping to once every eight weeks. Ah, the economic implications of style.

The Bottom Line: If you want to get ahead in corporate America—dress like a corporate gentleman. It can't hurt.

Avoid the Pitfalls of Business Casual

In the HBO comedy *Silicon Valley*, almost all the employees are running around in hoodies. Antonio Centeno, founder of *Real Men Real Style*, helps men leverage the science of style to command respect and build confidence. He correlates a sport coat to a "cure for cancer."[9] Here are a few tips on dressing for a more laid-back office environment:

- If you wear a sport coat and feel overdressed, unbutton it. Open it up and roll up the sleeves.

- Slim fit is for slimmer body types. Bigger body types should not wear skinny jeans. If you're a bigger guy, opt for a straight leg opening (not skinny) to balance you out.

- Find a brand that works for your body type. The fit matters more than the quality or the price.

That said, we all work in different industries—you may work at a technology company, and I may work at an investment bank. Doctors, construction workers, waiters, security guards, and soldiers all require uniforms. And that makes life easy. Apple's founder, Steve Jobs, agrees on the uniform idea. Jobs said he wanted to make all Apple employees wear the same vest.[10]

> Apple's founder, Steve Jobs, agrees on the uniform idea. Jobs said he wanted to make all Apple employees wear the same vest.

But not all jobs require a uniform.

Merely following the minimum dress code will not prequalify you for success. Like it or not, the truth is—you will immediately be sized up by colleagues based on how you dress. If someone comes up with the bright idea of dyeing his hair green to promote climate change at Amazon, do not dye yours. The importance of attire means you may feel unfairly judged and may also indicate that your office does not support a pure meritocracy. But this is reality, and it's not changing anytime soon.

It's a good idea to take note of what others are wearing during the interview process (when no one knows who you are). You don't have to carry a sign that says, "Hey, guys, does this suit work?" Look around and observe. Emulate the current executives and veteran employees.

Corporate Dress Code Policy

Now that Goldman Sachs bankers no longer have to show up at the office in a suit, a little confusion has occurred. This type of cultural change in a corporate setting has unleashed confusion over what to wear.

When it comes to working in an office, it's important that you dress appropriately (Secret Rule #8). If you don't dress appropriately and follow the company's dress code, then you may feel out of place. There's always pushback as dress standards change. Men might watch an episode of *Mad Men* and be tempted to think, *Why don't people dress like that anymore?* But there still are some fundamental standards.

- **A Tailored Fit.** First and foremost, wear clothes that fit properly. I can't stress this enough: fit is your most important consideration when buying dress clothes. Even the most expensive garment can appear haphazard if it doesn't complement your particular physique. If you are insecure about your body and wear ill-fitting clothes to hide certain parts, it will not help you—it compounds the issue, and you'll just look like a poorly dressed person who has something to hide. If you are overweight, that's okay—please don't try to wear a size too big or a size too small. Get sized by a professional.

- **Iron Your Clothes.** Having well-pressed clothing shows the world that you're a man of discipline and order, a man who has it all together and understands that details matter. It just feels good. Ironing isn't hard when you get the hang of it. If all else fails, you can always take it to the cleaners.

- **Shine Your Shoes.** Research shows that you can tell a lot about someone's personality, status, and income just by looking at his shoes.[11] Wear clean shoes, clean them regularly, take them in for a heel repair if they get worn, and don't run them into the ground. This is a typical bad habit. Just because your shoes are on the ground doesn't mean that no one sees them.

Mix It Up

Variety is important, but don't go too far—looking good is more important than wearing a new outfit every day. With that said, you should mix it up. Shop for accessories like ties, cuff links, belts, and socks on a regular basis. Your appearance is the selling point for yourself. In addition to the external benefits of dressing well, it's the most efficient way to broadcast to the office that you belong there, even if you don't feel that way. It gives you a chance to make some early mistakes without being harshly judged.

I have a friend, Mitchell, who interviewed for a technical position at a large telecom company in Dallas. This was not a client-facing position.

The job entailed hands-on work configuring network infrastructures. Mitchell was extremely smart, but he was also extremely introverted and terrified of meeting new people. Prior to the interview, we practiced role-playing for the meeting, and guess what aspect of the interview he was most nervous about? The fact that he had no idea what to wear to the interview. Out of all things!

If you're interviewing for a position, first and foremost, you need to understand the company's culture. Career coach Ryan Kahn, founder of The Hired Group, gives us a few ways to do this:

- If you have a contact who works inside the company, see if he or she can give you a heads-up about what people wear.

- If you don't have a contact, hang out in front of the office or sit in the coffee shop across the street to glimpse what people are wearing.

- You could also call the receptionist and ask: "I have an interview there next week. I don't want to be overdressed or too underdressed. What do you recommend?"[12]

Remember, almost all hiring decisions are formed in the first twenty seconds. Dressing well gives you a running start in every interview.

> Remember, almost all hiring decisions are formed in the first twenty seconds. Dressing well gives you a running start in every interview.

Corporate Etiquette for Men

Some things change, and some things never change.

Unfortunately, society is so splintered by cultural and political beliefs that there is no single set of universal manners and standards of etiquette being taught at home or in school. Most men have to figure it out on their own. This is why we need new corporate guidance, not just rules. Many men just aren't sure how to behave in the workplace anymore.

Bob, an engineer for a major automobile manufacturer in Warren, Michigan, told me that he had "no interest in becoming an executive manager." He liked his job. Bob was raised in a rural area of Michigan by a blue-collar family. He worked at the manufacturing plant, but since he was a top software engineer at the company, he still had to meet with senior management at corporate headquarters twice a year.

When Bob and his colleagues went out to eat, he recalled being mortified to learn that there were *eight* utensils at a formal dinner setting. "I only knew of three: a knife, a fork, and a spoon," he said. Isn't that funny? This is just one example of proper etiquette that you need to learn and learn fast. The author of *Hillbilly Elegy*, J. D. Vance, talks about his own lack of knowledge regarding corporate etiquette rules:

> I remember one in particular where I was at an event not too dissimilar from when I was trying to get a job at a fancy D.C. law firm, and I remember beforehand they had us corralled into this cocktail reception and a waitress came around and said, "Would you like some wine?" And I said: "Sure, I'll take some wine." She said, "Would you like red or white?" And I said, "I'll take some white wine." And then she said, "Do you like Chardonnay or Sauvignon Blanc?" And I actually remember thinking to myself, *This woman is screwing with me. Just give me some wine.*[1]

This may sound like an extreme example—at least for someone like Bob, a software engineer—but there are plenty of men from average college backgrounds who are navigating this type of unfamiliar territory in corporate America.

Elevate Your Pitch

Here's another awkward situation. My friend Jim is a web developer in Mountain View, California. It's an awesome place to work with fantastic benefits—like in-house massage rooms, free gourmet food, and fabulous retreats. There was minimal office gossip and a lot of camaraderie among the employees. Everyone was genuinely happy to work there. However, there was little interaction with senior management.

One day, Jim shared the elevator with one of the company's senior executives. As soon as he noticed who he was with, his palms became sweaty, his heart pounded, and his chest felt compressed. Anxiety took over. Although this was a perfect opportunity to meet the senior executive, Jim just froze.

Not only is there enormous pressure to speak with a Fortune 500 business leader, but an elevator ride complicates things—it means you also must speak fast, and get to the point quickly before it stops at their floor (unless you start pressing all the buttons).

Most of us have found ourselves in similar deep waters before—literally blindsided by the golden career opportunity of a lifetime—and froze. Words don't come out. Ideas in your head go blank. So, what can you say and what can you do?

Well, whatever you do, don't stay silent. At least make an introduction (Secret Rule #5). Push your nerves aside and say "hello." At a minimum: "Hi, Mrs. X. My name is Jim," and extend your hand. Don't start a conversation that would take a long time to finish or ask a question that would require a lengthy answer.

In sales, we practice our "elevator pitch." It's a thirty-second commercial you give to clients or prospects just in case you bump into them on your ride up to the office. You can mention what you do, who you work for, or a project that you just completed for the company.

Practice your elevator pitch. Role-play—in your office, at home, or at the gym in front of the mirror. Just kidding, don't do that. Preparation is more than half the battle. Know what you're going to say and how you're going to say it ahead of time. Use your imagination.

If memorizing a script doesn't fit your personality and you're afraid it won't seem authentic, then at least say something. Rather than launch into a script about yourself, tell that person how much you appreciate their work. Naturally, that person will want to know more about you, and then you can talk about yourself. But have some plan in mind so you don't freeze.

Mind Your P's and Q's

We have already discussed the importance of showing gratitude to your coworkers. But what about when you need something done? Saying "please" is the simplest thing you can do. Use the word *please* as often as you can.

> Saying "please" is the simplest thing you can do. Use the word *please* as often as you can.

It's also okay to sincerely say, "I'm sorry." And it's also okay to accept someone else's apology. A corporate gentleman knows when to keep his mouth shut and be conscious of other people's feelings, especially a woman's. Most of the time, you can avoid a painful situation by thinking before you speak (Secret Rule #7).

Sophia works in the marketing department for a retail grocer at its headquarters in Cincinnati, Ohio. Her coworker Richard had just reviewed the final draft of her proposal for the new downtown store, and they were ready to present it to their boss and the rest of the team. The new store featured a modern design with a sleek layout—a very different look compared to typical supermarkets.

During the presentation of the new store layout plans, Richard stole her ideas. He completely took over, dominating the presentation, and didn't give Sophia a chance to chime in. "When my boss turned to me for my input, there wasn't much else to say," she told me. Richard had thoroughly covered the entire proposal.

Sophia was obviously upset that he monopolized the entire presentation, so she developed a narrative that Richard downplayed her contributions because she was a woman. Whether or not this was true, instead of talking about it (or asking why he took all the credit for her work), she became completely distant and rude toward him. It created a tense and toxic work environment where tempers ran hot. The team's productivity was reduced by 23 percent and, even worse, it made the office a hostile place to work.

This issue could have easily been avoided by saying something like, "I'm sorry, I had no idea I was rambling on," or "I shouldn't have dominated the presentation, it was inconsiderate." And all this could have been avoided if Richard had just been a little more thoughtful and minded his p's and q's. Hey, what happened to "ladies go first"?

Check Your Ego

A gentleman never asks an employee to make his coffee. If you drink coffee, learn how to operate the coffee machine yourself. There is a big difference between confidence and narcissism.

There are two kinds of pride—there's just plain old pride in one's work and one's life accomplishments, and then there is foolish pride. This is an inflated, egotistical, look-at-me pride. In fact, being a narcissist often projects a lack of confidence or an abundance of overconfidence. Excessive pride is usually a form of compensation for deep feelings of inferiority.

> There are two kinds of pride—there's just plain old pride in one's work and one's life accomplishments, and then there is foolish pride.

Do you really have to pat yourself on the back in front of your employees? Don't they see you at work every day, and aren't they part of your accomplishments? You're a team! Don't let a little pride turn into ego. No one wants to work with a showboat or get sidelined from the project because someone won't share the spotlight presenting your new healthcare plan or your new overtime policy.

Many women I interviewed told me they were "consistently repelled by overbearing and conceited men." Hence, *narcissists*. A woman who works for one of the largest logistic shippers in Memphis, Tennessee, told me she hates working for an overbearing boss. A conceited manager makes her feel anxious, because he assumes (in her experience) that he knows what she wants. Never *assume* anything.

No Bullying Allowed

One more thing. As we discussed in Chapter 11, bullying in the workplace affects both men and women. Research reveals that nearly 75 percent of employees have been affected by workplace bullying.[2] According to SHRM, "bullying is the repeated, health-harming mistreatment of one or more persons (the targets) by one or more perpetrators. **Bullying** is abusive conduct that is threatening, humiliating or intimidating or work-interference—that is, sabotage—which prevents work from being done."[3]

> "Bullying is abusive conduct that is threatening, humiliating or intimidating or work-interference—that is, sabotage—which prevents work from being done."

Workplace bullying is four times more prevalent than workplace sexual harassment or racial discrimination. It's unacceptable. It's one of the Seven Deadly Sins in Chapter 11. It negatively affects overall morale in the workplace. How can your subordinates do their best work and exceed expectations if they live in fear?

If you're still unsure of how to act in an inclusive workplace, watch the movie *The Intern*. Throughout the film, Ben, the intern (played by Robert De Niro), shows viewers what he has learned in his life—from dressing well to always having a handkerchief available for any issue, like a woman's tears. His boss, Jules (played by Anne Hathaway), is the chief executive officer of a start-up retail company, an industry still dominated by men, and struggles to make her company successful.

Blessed with the wisdom of his generation, De Niro plays a type of magical sage who brings a gentlemanly approach to the workplace. The benefits extend much further than just his behavior toward women—he uplifts the spirits of other coworkers and motivates the entire office.

Influencing Your Corporate Culture

You have the power to influence your workplace culture.

"Culture eats strategy for breakfast."
—Peter Drucker

Corporate culture could be described as the character of the company—its management, its employees, and the type of customer it attracts. Every year, the *Wall Street Journal* releases a list of the best-managed companies and explains how they got that way. A team of researchers at Claremont Graduate University's Drucker Institute compiles the list using dozens of data points to evaluate companies on five performance dimensions: customer satisfaction, employee engagement and development, innovation, social responsibility, and financial strength. Here are some that make the cut—Amazon, Alphabet (Google), Cisco Systems, Johnson & Johnson, Hewlett Packard, and Procter & Gamble. If you work for a company that's on this list, consider yourself lucky.[1]

When you like where you work, it's not just beneficial to your mental as well as physical health; it's also good for the corporation. Unfortunately, far too many people don't like where they work, both men and women. According to an article in the *Harvard Business Review* called "The Leader's Guide to Corporate Culture," **culture** is the implied social order of an organization. It shapes attitudes and behaviors in wide-ranging and durable ways. Cultural norms define what is encouraged, discouraged, accepted, or rejected within a social group.

> Culture is the tacit social order of an organization. It shapes attitudes and behaviors in wide-ranging and durable ways. Cultural norms define what is encouraged, discouraged, accepted, or rejected within a social group.

A cultural fit is important. When properly aligned with personal values and needs, culture can unleash tremendous amounts of energy toward a shared purpose and foster an organization's capacity to thrive. What are some things that determine a good fit?

- Shared enthusiasm about a company's mission or purpose
- A common approach to working together
- A mutual understanding of how to make decisions and assess risk

Today, more young employees are holding their employers accountable for their values and insisting that the company stand for something. In *The Culture Engine,* author Chris Edmonds said, "Seven percent of young workers surveyed by Deloitte say they dislike their employer's corporate culture so much that they intend to quit their jobs in the next two years."[2]

> "Seven percent of young workers surveyed by Deloitte say they dislike their employer's corporate culture so much that they intend to quit their jobs in the next two years."

I once fell in that category, so I get it. This is one reason your company's culture is very important. Growing employee activism is marked by walkouts protesting employers' stances on everything from environmental issues to immigration policies. All of this promises to put more CEOs in the hot seat, as we discussed in Chapter 2. As employees become more vocal, executives will have to listen. This is the main reason your company's corporate culture is very important, and it doesn't just come from the top.

Influencing Culture as an Employee

Every employee contributes to the workplace culture, and therefore every employee can have some influence to change it. Consider Daryl, an employee for one of the biggest US conglomerates. He worked as a database administrator for various departments. During COVID-19, his department was in the middle of laying off employees after a challenging quarter. Daryl knew that he had no control over the ultimate outcome; he could only control how he handled himself during this tumultuous time. So, he decided that the best thing to do was maintain a genuinely positive attitude and help as many people as he could. During the layoffs, he was a calming voice and an inspiration to many of his coworkers.

Your company's culture can improve if you make it your mission to provide positive feedback to your coworkers. Even if you're not a manager, you can recognize your colleagues for a job well done. Show appreciation for their efforts (as we discussed in Chapter 5). Everyone wants to be acknowledged for their hard work. This proves true even if it's just a kind word given in passing.

As an employee, it can be frustrating to see a need for change, while not having the authority to make things happen. But you do have influence. If you have specific concerns about the corporate culture, raise those concerns with your manager. If it's involving the manager, go to human resources.

> If you have specific concerns about the corporate culture, raise those concerns with your manager. If it's involving the manager, go to human resources.

Follow the policy handbook—the process for escalating concerns and engaging others who can make change happen. As I learned in a prior job, the dividing line between HR and management is not always clear in every company.

As an employee, you can influence culture in small ways by making connections with your superiors. Compliment your manager and leverage those relationships to inspire the change you seek. Make constructive suggestions about social outings or community work, which can happen outside the office. Both managers and employees have the power to set a tone that encourages feedback.

Influencing Culture as a Manager

According to Deloitte, only 19 percent of CEOs and HR leaders felt they had the right culture.[3]

> Only 19 percent of CEOs and HR leaders felt they had the right culture.

Quite often, the bigger a corporation gets, the colder it becomes. One way to warm it up is to remember people's names and give employees the recognition they deserve. The ability of managers to handle people is what makes them successful. Here's one manager who does a good job of that:

Daniel Lubetsky is the chief executive officer of the snack company KIND. Lubetsky has always aimed to use his leadership to foster kindness and compassion throughout the company. In order to truly practice what he preached, Lubetsky started the "Kindos" initiative, which encourages any employee to recognize a colleague's act of kindness by sending an email to the team. Managers also carry "#kindawesome cards" to hand out to anyone they see doing something generous. "It sounds simple, but it helps people celebrate and more regularly spot opportunities to be good humans," Lubetsky told *Forbes*. "It also helps everyone in our community feel like co-owners, much as we would in a family."[4]

This is one easy and impactful act of inspiration in corporate culture that works. Again, corporate culture is largely driven by how those corporate leaders behave. A company's leaders may be very smart and hardworking, but if they aren't thoughtful and kind, there is a good chance the company will not be inclusive. As more companies see the effect that mindful culture has on their productivity and bottom line, they will look to promote those who are instrumental in creating that culture faster.

What thoughtfulness doesn't mean is that everyone in your office needs to wear kid gloves around one another. The goal is for both genders to work together more comfortably and effectively. Another way to do this is to encourage employee feedback and maintain an anonymous online portal for constant feedback.

These small and simple changes can make a big difference. Does your company have a culture where people like to work? What do others outside of your company say or think about your culture? Is it inclusive?

If you are in a position to hire employees, the most important thing you can do to create a positive corporate culture is to focus on hiring people who fit the mold of the culture you want to create. For example, people who are easy and open to work with, and people who are supportive of others.

In corporate America, some employers use a personality test before they hire a candidate. **The Myers–Briggs Type Indicator** is one of those tests. Deborah Borg, an HR and communications professional for an architecture firm in upstate New York, sees personality tests as tools to evaluate both current employees and job candidates.[5] One of the most famous measurements of the Myers–Briggs Type Indicator is Type A versus Type B personalities.

If you're a Type A: You're driven and organized.

If you're a Type B: You're laid back and adaptable.

This analysis has its roots in the 1950s American tobacco industry, where cigarette companies invented Type A as a high-strung target demographic, people who needed to buy cigarettes right away to help take the edge off.

However, the Myers–Briggs Type Indicator does have limitations. Alisa Cohn, an executive coach based in New York City who's administered hundreds of personality tests, said many of these tests simply highlight preferences, not necessarily skills you do or don't have.[6] It cannot uncover all of a candidate's psychological traits for employers to make an informed hiring decision. Therefore, some new employee personality traits you just have to learn how to deal with after that person is hired. And society deems "toxic masculinity" to be one of them.

"Toxic Masculinity" in the Workplace

The financial sector fares worst in terms of sexual harassment allegations. A Merrill Lynch employee sued the firm after she said she was subject to discrimination and sexual harassment that included colleagues making sexual jokes and clients "asking her to sit on their laps."[7] According to a survey by SourceMedia, one-third of women in the wealth management industry reported a "high prevalence of sexual misconduct" in the workplace.[8]

> One-third of women in the wealth management industry reported a "high prevalence of sexual misconduct" in the workplace.

Toxic masculinity refers to harmful attitudes about how "real men" should act. It fuels antiquated notions—such as men should suppress certain emotions—and in a workplace context, it encourages hypercompetitiveness, posturing, and a need to appear dominant.[9]

Toxic masculinity is the idea that there is only one way to be a man. It means that anyone who doesn't fit this stereotype of a strong man is somehow less valuable, and anyone who displays stereotypical feminine traits will be less successful. Of course that's not true!

The term *masculinity* itself is dynamic, not static. There is no "right" way to be a man. Not all men fit a standard mold of manhood—many men are struggling with their sexual identity or have been subjected to discriminatory comments or violence from other men.

Both men and women can be aggressive; they simply express aggression differently. This whole idea of toxic masculinity is premised on a peer pressure model—the idea that men do bad things. For example, treating women badly or punching someone in the face, just because other men will cheer them on. Masculinity is fine. It's when it becomes intolerant of either women or men with different interests that it becomes "toxic."

The editor of *GQ* magazine's "New Masculinity," Will Welch, said: This issue is an exploration of the ways that traditional notions of masculinity are being challenged, shifted, and overturned. It's also intended as an exploration of how we can all become more generous, honest, open, and loving humans—especially if we rebuild masculinity on a foundation of traits and values like generosity, honesty, openness, and love.

Anyone who believes that bullying, harassment, and shaming are specific to men has clearly never met a teenage girl.

> Anyone who believes that bullying, harassment, and shaming are specific to men has clearly never met a teenage girl.

And guess what? Women are not the sole victims of "toxic masculinity" in the workplace. Men can be affected by it just as much. Even if men are not directly targeted, the culture can force men to suppress their own feelings in order to fit in with narrow expectations of masculinity at work.

Thankfully, few forms of masculinity are toxic for the workplace, but just in case, I laid out rules on how to be a gentleman in today's inclusive workplace in Chapter 10. If you're a manager, here are some other ideas:

- **Listen to your employees.** One of the simplest ways to protect yourself from a negative perception at work is to listen more. Make a conscious effort not to talk over your employees, even if you don't agree with them. In meetings, strive to give every-one equal time to talk. Not everyone will be as assertive or as loud as the dominant voices in the room.

- **Ask your employees for help.** Nothing facilitates collaboration more than asking for assistance. It shows you value the input of others and aren't a narcissist. If someone does help you out, afford that person the credit she deserves. Some competition can help productivity, but too much of it can lead to hostility—people stop communicating effectively, learning from one an-other, and working toward the same goal.

- **Assess your behavior toward your female colleagues.** Be hon-est. Do you sometimes address the men in a meeting before the women? Do you make judgments based on a woman's appear-ance in a way you wouldn't with a man? Do you make assump-tions about a woman's interests or hobbies based on traditional gender norms? Are you more comfortable getting feedback from your male colleagues than your female colleagues?

Regardless of your own personal beliefs, there is more than one way to be a man. And more than one way to become an effective manager. Masculinity itself isn't toxic. Conflict resolution skills can help you un-derstand and change the roots of any toxic-generated behavior in the workplace.

Microaggressions and Unconscious Bias

You have a new responsibility—not just policing your own behavior, but that of your subordinates and coworkers. Most people are not con-sciously or intentionally prejudiced in the workplace. Most people want to behave ethically and in an unbiased manner too. Yet two decades of research actually reveals that we all have biases.

Why do you suppose that is? According to Timothy Wilson, professor of psychology at the University of Virginia, it's due to the amount of information our brains are faced with at any given moment.[10] Eleven million pieces of information, to be exact. And guess how many bits of information the brain can process at one time? Only forty.

To compensate for the millions of pieces that go unprocessed, your brain uses shortcuts and past knowledge to make assumptions. For instance, when you pick up your cell phone, you know it's a cell phone without having to catalog each of its parts and search your memories to discover what it is and what it's used for—you get to skip straight through to checking your email. Some may call that efficient. Psychologists call it *unconscious bias*. In the *Harvard Business Review*, academics Stefanie Johnson, Ksenia Keplinger, Jessica Kirk, and Liza Barnes state that:

> Organizations should also pay attention to gender harassment, including bullying and sexist comments about women. Offering training on microaggressions and on unconscious bias could be useful not only for encouraging civil behavior but also for empowering peers and leaders to step in when they see bullying and harassing behavior in the workplace. It can be stressful for a woman to stand up to sexist comments when they are directed at her, but it can be a lot easier for a bystander to step in and diffuse the situation.[11]

But what exactly are *microaggressions* and *unconscious bias*? According to *Business Insider*, **microaggressions** are "unconscious expressions of racism or sexism. They come out in seemingly innocuous comments by people who might be well intentioned."[12]

> Microaggressions are "unconscious expressions of racism or sexism. They come out in seemingly innocuous comments by people who might be well intentioned."

For example, asking an Asian coworker where she is "really from" is a microaggression. Why? Because it could imply that the person you are speaking to isn't American and doesn't belong here. Or maybe you are just being friendly and asking about her background, taking a genuine interest. Unfortunately, in the modern workplace, it doesn't matter what you meant. What matters is how your coworker interpreted it. Don't let things get lost in translation. Put yourself in their shoes. If you can't empathize with others, you will never be successful.

Interrupting is another microaggression, frequently directed at women. Research reveals that women are much more frequently interrupted than men. A study conducted by George Washington University found that men interrupted women 33 percent more often than they interrupt other men.[13]

But some argue that the whole concept of microaggressions in the workplace has gone too far, even the professor who originally popularized the term. Derald Wing Sue is a professor of psychology at Columbia University. Sue is concerned that people have missed the point. It should not be about shaming or punishing people. In fact, people who commit microaggressions are not necessarily racist or sexist at all. As he told the *Chronicle of Higher Education*: "People who engage in microaggressions are oftentimes well-intentioned, decent individuals who aren't aware that they are engaging in an offensive way toward someone else."

> "People who engage in microaggressions are oftentimes well-intentioned, decent individuals who aren't aware that they are engaging in an offensive way toward someone else."

Sue goes on to say, "I'm glad employers have found the research useful, but I am cautious about corporations that are taking it as an absolute."[14] Joking around a little bit and cutting up with coworkers is not what it used to be, and that's okay.

According to studies at the University of California, **unconscious biases** are "social stereotypes about certain groups of people that individuals form outside their own conscious awareness. Everyone holds unconscious beliefs about various social and identity groups, and these biases stem from one's tendency to organize social worlds by categorizing."[15]

This is referring to judgment—the "don't judge a book by its cover" notion. Let's try something. Here's a test: read the following statements and answer them as quickly as you can. What is the very first thing that comes to mind? Be honest. Go!

- At work, women tend to _____
- My female coworker is a _____
- The #MeToo movement is _____
- Compared to boys, girls are _____

Interesting, right? Researchers from Columbia's Business School conducted a study called the Heidi/Howard Roizen case. For the case study, students were asked to review and then evaluate a man's résumé—an executive named Howard Roizen.[16] "He worked at Apple, launched his own software company, and had been a partner at a venture capital firm. He was a proficient networker and had very powerful friends, including Bill Gates." The students concluded he would be an excellent person to hire because he was someone who got things done and was (obviously) very likable.

Shockingly, the exact same résumé was evaluated by other students, only it used a woman's name, Heidi Roizen. And what was the conclusion? The students' appraisal of Heidi was dramatically different from their appraisal of Howard! They said Heidi was more selfish and less desirable than Howard, even though the résumés reflected the exact same credentials.

So, what can you do about microaggressions and unconscious biases? As far as unconscious biases—try to think more deeply about your own background and your beliefs. Perhaps some of your most deeply held beliefs simply aren't true. The mark of a true leader, colleague, and gentleman is having the humility to examine one's own beliefs and admit that they might be wrong.

Regarding microaggressions—if you're tempted to ask someone where they are from or if you feel like interrupting a female colleague at a meeting, the easiest thing to do is to keep your mouth shut, or you may end up in court, or at least the HR department.

As an employee, you must think critically. In the workplace, it is important to understand when you may be relying on impulses driven by an unconscious bias and to challenge those thoughts. When you do this, you have the power to make a better-informed and inclusive decision for both men and women.

Conflict Management

Men experience more interoffice conflict than women.[17] In order to create a culture where people like to work, conflict management skills are crucial. As a supervisor, one of your duties is to give sincere assessments about where employees shine and where they need improvement. This can be a tricky task for managers. For example, a man may make light of a woman's negative feelings and say, "Ah, don't worry about it." To another man, this phrase may seem friendly. But to a female coworker, this statement can come across as insensitive and uncaring. (Remember our differences in Chapter 4?)

In the current era of microaggressions, a lot of managers are having a difficult time giving valuable feedback to women. The share of male managers who said they were uncomfortable participating in common job-related activities with women, such as mentoring, working together, or socializing together, is a growing concern. According to the *Wall Street Journal*, 60 percent of senior men say they hesitate to work with a junior woman.[18]

> In the current era of microaggressions, a lot of managers are having a difficult time giving valuable feedback to women.

Receiving constructive criticism from your boss is a key to getting ahead and growing at work. But Elisabeth Kelan, a professor of leadership, says that giving candid feedback to anybody can be tough for managers who want to avoid conflict or don't have the time. The lack of constructive feedback to women employees frequently stems from concern about appearing biased or being too harsh. "There's this fear that if you give a woman honest feedback, she will break out in tears, that women need to be protected," she said. And "that's just not the case."[19]

And what makes it even tougher? Due to historical realities, women are more likely to exhibit a victim mentality at work than a man. A cognitive psychologist in Mclean, Virginia, told me that some women may commit what's known as a **Fundamental Attribution Error**: judging a man's character as automatically "bad" just because he is a man, without seeing one's own behavior as unreasonable.

Stephen R. Covey's *The 7 Habits of Highly Effective People* notes a serious problem with reactive language—it becomes a self-fulfilling prophecy. True or not, people accept the paradigm they've created as truth, and then seek specific evidence to support that belief. They feel increasingly victimized and out of control, not in charge of their life or their destiny. They blame outside forces for their situation. In other words, it's a tendency to carry over attitudes from the days of "my dog ate my homework" or "my daddy is bigger than your daddy."

Some managers may find that a lot of employees don't welcome critiques or even constructive criticism. This is disappointing, because employment growth only occurs if employees are open to constructive feedback. And it's even more difficult to reason with a "victim." Have you heard the expression, you just can't win an argument with a woman? (*Only kidding here.*)

While completing a public speaking course, the director of the program told us that the key to winning any debate was to proactively call out the opponent's attacks and grievances first. Beat them to the punch. Address the issue and then move on with your argument. Connect on an emotional level.

Connect on an Emotional Level

I cannot emphasize this point enough—connect on an emotional level. This is the secret to creating a long-lasting, successful, and inclusive workplace culture. Unfortunately, many companies value logic over emotions. They don't consider how employees feel, because that's what HR is for. The more closely aligned you are with your employees' feelings, the more likely you are to create an inclusive environment.

> The more closely aligned you are with your employees' feelings, the more likely you are to create an inclusive environment.

An example of this occurred when Cisco chief executive officer Chuck Robbins sent a company-wide email about the importance of prioritizing mental health, asking his seventy-five thousand employees to "talk openly and extend compassion" to one another and encouraging them to seek professional help if needed. He never expected the overwhelming response. More than one hundred employees replied to his email, opening up about their own mental health struggles. Realizing the problem was widespread, Robbins worked to provide his employees with anxiety and depression screenings, meditation and yoga classes, counseling for employees and their families, and on-site treatment and health centers.[20]

Here's another good example: Tony Hsieh, the chief executive officer of Zappos, knows how to connect to employees on an emotional level. He lets them know the company is much more than just a retail shoe business. Why? Because Hsieh fosters a corporate culture built around customer service above all else. He uses methods to inspire his employees to uphold this dedication. For example, when employees perform exceptional customer service, they ring a bell in the office. Everyone then cheers them on. This validates an employee, boosts morale, and reinforces how they can continue to contribute to the company's underlying goal.[21]

You can implement validation techniques like this as a way to excite and inspire employees to see the company's vision and work harder to make it come true.

How Your Employer Can Help You

We're all in this together.

S martBrief polled readers to gauge top priorities in the workplace. One question was, "Which human resources trend do you think employees should care about most and why?"[1] Here's what employees had to say:

- Leadership
- Employee morale
- Engagement

If you search for the most popular workplace stories that engage readers, the stories that rise to the top are those that expose poor leadership and toxic environments, but "eliminating sexual harassment and workplace misconduct" accounted for only 4.2 percent of responses.

How can employers make your life easier as a man in the inclusive modern workplace? By offering initiatives that open opportunities for growth, such as leadership-development programs or professional learning courses. These are the types of programs employees say help them feel valued by and connected to their employers.

Human Resources Empowerment

Love 'em or hate 'em, the human resources department can help you. Not only can HR help guide your career, they can help you protect your job. Along with the workforce and the economy, the role of an HR professional has changed, and the evolution will continue as machines and technology replace tasks once performed by humans. But that doesn't make you or your job less important today.

Jill Goldstein works for talent and HR operations at management consulting firm Accenture. Goldstein said: "I can envision a future where HR professionals are no longer thinking that their job is to stay on top of current HR trends, but to reposition (themselves) to become workforce advisors."[2]

> "I can envision a future where HR professionals are no longer thinking that their job is to stay on top of current HR trends, but to reposition (themselves) to become workforce advisors."

Instead of thinking of HR as the enemy, find a way to leverage HR's job to help advance your career. In Chapter 9, we outlined the case for an HR department's purpose—to protect the company, not you. While that may be true, there are ways you can benefit from their assistance. According to the Society for Human Resource Management (SHRM), many companies are ditching the title "HR manager" for titles like chief happiness officer, director of talent-attraction strategy, and even head of positive people. At Cisco, Executive Vice President Fran Katsoudas's title changed from HR officer to chief people officer.[3]

SHRM published a report, "HR 2025: 7 Critical Strategies to Prepare for the Future of HR," authored by Susan Milligan, who states: "The 2025 workforce will include not just transient workers, but also gig workers who pop in and out of jobs on a daily basis. In addition, HR will need to help assess which tasks throughout the organization can be automated and then reskill those whose jobs are affected by automation."[4]

> "The 2025 workforce will include not just transient workers, but also gig workers who pop in and out of jobs on a daily basis. In addition, HR will need to help assess which tasks throughout the organization can be automated and then reskill those whose jobs are affected by automation."

We've explored the role of corporate inclusiveness training and policies in changing corporate culture. They are necessary tools, but they only take a company so far, especially in the wake of the discomfort that so many men now feel working alongside women in the workplace. In fact, Cindy Robbins, president and chief people officer of Salesforce, reports, "The number of men who are uncomfortable mentoring women has tripled. . . . Some men are avoiding women altogether in the workplace, from not including female colleagues in business travel to avoiding one-on-one meetings."[5]

This type of behavior is not only detrimental to a woman's career, it's gender discrimination. At the World Economic Forum, the global organization noted that employers needed to more fully support men in their efforts to change discriminatory behavior. In fact, for those in a position to propose policies, hire personnel, and promote personnel, data tells a powerful story of what is currently happening in any corporate environment. By asking for data connected to gender, supervisors can more fully understand where imbalances in pay, hiring, and promotion exist and take steps to fix those imbalances. Ensuring that access to data is available is one powerful step HR can take to ensure that all supervisors are aware of the status quo and can take data-driven steps to address any inconsistencies surrounding gender.

How an Employer Can Help Employees

As a small-business owner, the inclusion and expansion of female hires can have a positive impact on your bottom line. Having a diverse team leads to increased innovation and creative thinking, not only a broader appeal to your customers. A bigger reach to your consumers means a bigger boost to your profits. It also improves decision making and your ability to identify and resolve issues before they occur. Here are five ways an employer can help facilitate a successful, inclusive environment:

1. Educate on Bias

As we discussed in Chapter 15, bias is subtle. So subtle, in fact, that you can convince yourself that you aren't biased when you are. Don't feel bad—we all engage in bias. It's a behavior that's not only hard to recognize, but also hard to change. Therefore, HR can help all employees to recognize and overcome biases that lead to less-than-inclusive workplaces. Inc.com offered a useful list of biases that are likely to affect the workplace, especially when it comes to gender and racial issues.[6] Some of these biases include:

- **Perception bias:** The tendency to form stereotypes and assumptions about certain groups that make objective decision making impossible.

- **Affinity bias:** The tendency to gravitate toward people who remind us of ourselves.

- **Halo effect:** The tendency to always see someone in a positive light because of their title or because you like them.

- **Groupthink:** The tendency for people to go along with the group rather than voicing their individual thoughts and beliefs.

Everyone needs help in identifying their own biases, because most biases are unconscious. Once they are identified, training continues to help individuals understand why their biases are harmful, how to recognize them in action, and how to counteract them.

Tayo Rockson, president and chief executive officer at UYD Management, said: "One of the things that impacts our ability to connect effectively across cultures is unconscious bias. It affects who we are as individuals and the decisions we make. Since individuals make up systems—and by extension institutions and policies—it is imperative that we commit to being aware of our biases so they don't limit our thinking."[7]

> "One of the things that impacts our ability to connect effectively across cultures is unconscious bias."

For gender-based bias to change, company leadership, managers, and rank-and-file employees must all be committed. Steps that can be taken on a corporate-wide or individual department basis include:

- Avoiding gender-based language
- Using anonymized résumés
- Following a standardized interview template
- Engaging in collaborative decision making with a diverse group of people

I really like the idea of **anonymizing** (or blinding) résumés. It's a step taken so that the reviewer cannot see the name or background of the applicants they are assessing. This enables hirers to make the best possible decision, which often results in more diverse and inclusive corporate cultures. One HR professional told me they have hired this way (anonymizing) for years now and would "never, ever go back."

Doing this in conjunction with group discussions and problem solving helps raise awareness of biases and encourages a solution-oriented mindset in regard to gender bias.[8]

2. Align Actions with Policies

All too often, little changes in response to corporate policies, because those policies are selectively enforced. Tech goliath Google is a perfect example, paying a total of $105 million to two senior executives accused of sexual harassment.[9] When anti–sexual harassment and gender-bias policies are not only implemented, but actually enforced, employees can be more confident that their company believes in gender equity.

3. Form an Inclusion Council

The Society for Human Resource Management recommends the formation of an inclusion council composed of eight to twelve senior leaders one or two steps below the CEO.[10] When such a council is made up of committed individuals who truly want to change corporate culture, it can represent a powerful force for change. It's helpful for men in the workplace to see men in leadership who they admire actively participating in such an endeavor, because it models the behavior that will ultimately change what happens in a company on a day-to-day basis.

What's the job of an inclusion council? They typically are active in the following areas:

- Setting goals around gender inclusivity in hiring, retention, and promotions
- Addressing engagement issues among underrepresented employee groups
- Building a case for diversity and inclusion across a company
- Creating messaging about the positive impact of gender inclusion
- Identifying inclusive training and education opportunities

4. Fairer Employee Evaluations

When supervisors use outdated evaluation forms and protocols, there's little incentive or ability to change outdated evaluation practices.[11] Unstructured evaluations can lead to and/or perpetuate bias, because they don't offer an alternative to evaluating employees based on unbiased metrics.

Removing subjectivity from performance evaluations translates to fairer treatment, so that promotions and recognition are based on merit, rather than favoritism. HR can provide significant help for male supervisors who must evaluate their employees by offering not only unbiased evaluation tools, but also promoting training based on those tools. However, even the best performance and evaluation tools must be used correctly for them to function effectively. A fair evaluation and promotion system works best when supervisors clearly state to their direct reports what their expectations are and how those can be met.

Michael Schneider, a human capital specialist, said: "To hedge your risks, articulate your expectations and clarify your requirements to your colleagues—especially when defining what success looks like in a role and what constitutes successful performance."[12]

> "To hedge your risks, articulate your expectations and clarify your requirements to your colleagues—especially when defining what success looks like in a role and what constitutes successful performance."

5. Encourage Inclusion Resource Groups

More than 90 percent of Fortune 500 companies include groups that bring together employees with different types of commonalities. To be effective, such groups must emerge organically from within. However, there are steps that employers can take to facilitate the formation and growth of these types of groups for the purposes of encouraging inclusivity.

Companies can make it as easy as possible for these groups to meet by offering time off to employees to attend meetings and providing a central meeting place that's easy to access and comfortable. Highlighting gender inclusion in employee newsletters can help with the growth of such groups as well as provide a corporate "seal of approval." Senior managers can support these groups by speaking at their meetings and participating in networking opportunities. HR and company leaders can also actively tap these groups for intelligence on their preferred professional development activities.

Finally, inclusion employee resource groups can provide the opportunity for women to learn new skills in a risk-free environment through development programs and workshops. Such activities can help women develop marketable skills to help them advance within a company, building a gender-inclusive workplace from the ground up.

Peaceful Coexistence
in the Inclusive Workplace

There is a true synergy that comes from working together.

There is a true synergy that comes from men and women working together, and in doing so they create far more value than either can create alone. Goldman Sachs has a *10,000 Women* initiative to help fund female business owners, yet almost 80 percent of senior leaders are male.[1] According to Joanne Lipman, author of *That's What She Said*:

> Evidence proves that women actually achieve better financial results than their male counterparts. Female-led funds outperform those run by men by a large margin. The same is true for banks with female CEOs or board chairs. One study found that male-led banks were six to seven times more likely to fail during financial crisis than those led by women.[2]

Our biological and hormonal differences don't mean that one sex is better or smarter than the other; it simply explains some of our behaviors.

• • •

Gender Preferences Are Changing

In my experience, I've found that most men simply aren't sure how to handle a powerful woman. If a woman is emasculating you at work, it could actually stem from her own weakness. Her insecurity is the only rational reason for behaving like this. But, you can't change her; you can only change yourself. So, what's the good news? Times *are* changing.

For the first time ever, Americans' preference about the gender of their boss is changing. A majority, 55 percent, say their boss's gender makes no difference to them.[3]

> For the first time ever, Americans' preference about the gender of their boss is changing. A majority, 55 percent, say their boss's gender makes no difference to them.

The shift away from Americans preferring a male boss suggests that employees may be reacting to the stream of sexual harassment allegations against men in workplaces across many industries, from Hollywood to Capitol Hill. As high-profile men accused of sexual harassment in the workplace resign or are fired, employers consider replacing them with women. Regardless, people should be able to like where they work. Again, quite often, people don't quit companies, they quit their bosses.

Women have risen to the top and broken the "glass ceiling." According to the *Intuit 2020 Report: Twenty Trends That Will Shape the Next Decade:* "In the industrialized world, women will continue making educational, economic and political advancements." The outlook is for a **she-economy**—a term that represents the near-billion women who will be new economic contributors. And the gender pay gap will soon become a thing of the past.[4]

> "In the industrialized world, women will continue making educational, economic and political advancements."

With more women taking part in the workforce than ever before, it's only natural to expect a shift in office dynamics.

Sexism Is on the Decline

According to the US Equal Employment Opportunity Commission (EEOC), discrimination charges (like sexism) are down, while sexual harassment charges have risen. However, the EEOC noted the impact of societal developments on the increase in claims: "We cannot look back without noting the significant impact of the #MeToo movement in the number of sexual harassment charges filed with the agency."[5] In other words, the reason for the increase may be that more people feel comfortable speaking out—not necessarily an indication that issues of workplace harassment have actually increased.

According to CBS News, high-profile incidents of sexual harassment have actually declined.[6] With some notable exceptions, like Harvey Weinstein and his "casting couch" approach to Hollywood movie hires, most harassment claims focus on a "hostile workplace environment" fact pattern, rather than the old-fashioned, quid-pro-quo story of men holding promotions hostage to sexual favors. A study from Leeds University also found that workplace sexual harassment claims have declined, and the feeling of isolation reported by those claims has lessened.[7]

> Workplace sexual harassment claims have declined, and the feeling of isolation reported by those claims has lessened.

Retaliation is the most frequently filed charge of job discrimination nationwide—in fact, retaliation accounts for more than half of all EEOC charges.[8] Given these statistics, it is not terribly surprising that employees are anxious about what might happen to them if they report misconduct or concerns at work.

While the feminist movement has helped advance women in the workforce, in many cases, the pendulum may have swung too far (see

Chapter 3). There has been a significant drop in sexual harassment, men exhibiting sexism, and male leadership exerting pressure on women based on gender. And things will continue to improve. This doesn't mean sexual harassment no longer occurs in the workplace—it's just less frequent and more subtle.

A Fair Shot

While this book focuses on diversity or inclusivity from a gender perspective—there is no place in the office for harassment or ill treatment of any hired hand, whether that person be a secretary or your boss. Whether it is a man or a woman, everyone should be treated with respect (Secret Rule #12). Employees emptying the trash cans and cleaning the bathrooms at night deserve the most respect. Imagine the utter chaos if they all suddenly went on strike.

If you're still not exactly sure what harassment is, refer back to Chapter 2. Practice the Golden Rule: "Do unto others as you would have them do unto you." Good relationships will develop and have a positive impact on the company's bottom line. When worries of bad employee behavior are minimal to nonexistent, a company's vision and purpose are enabled to reach its maximum potential.

Even the Dalai Lama apologized for controversial comments about the possibility of a woman succeeding him. When speaking to the BBC, the Tibetan spiritual leader said that, "Any future female Dalai Lama should be attractive."[9] His office had to issue a formal apology, explaining that he was only "joking."

Sometimes, everyone sees interaction a little differently. And so, unintentional mistakes can occur, but the suggestions outlined in this book can help you prevent them.

Like most men, most women want a chance to do the best job they can to help support their families and make use of their skills. They want to go to work and do their jobs without being hassled, and either go home to their families or outside social circle. There is a lot that can go wrong mixing up these two worlds—your work life and your personal life—and despite the prevalence of Instagram and social media, the smartest people are building a firewall between them.

By understanding that all (most) women want is a fair shot (as discussed in Chapter 4) without a lot of hassle, you can relate better at work. And this includes thinking before you act. I'm asking that you take a few minutes to think about the consequences before you stare at the new assistant's chest or dare to send a flirty text to the new sales rep. Think how you would feel if someone directed those actions at your daughter, your wife, or even your mom.

The Bottom Line: The vast majority of women aren't interested in taking you down or giving you crap—if you treat them with respect, they'll do the same for you.

You Have the Power

You actually do a lot of things right already, but it's the little things in life that really matter. Your female coworkers will notice when you make an effort on their behalf, and they will really appreciate it.

As we outlined in Chapter 15, you have the power to influence your workplace environment. How does your current corporate culture impact employees? You owe it to your colleagues to ensure that your workplace behavior does not make them feel uncomfortable, unsafe, or unequal. You owe it to your colleagues to recognize and correct any bad behavior and to show your female colleagues that you believe it's the right thing to do. Also, doing the right thing should keep you out of trouble and give you a sense of job security.

Men need to understand the perceptions of women in the workplace and create a climate where both can peacefully and comfortably exist. A Pew Research Center poll revealed that 66 percent of adults age sixty-five and older believe it's now harder for men to navigate workplace interactions. The survey also indicated the majority of Americans believe the increased focus on sexual harassment has made it more difficult for men to know how to interact with women at work.[10]

> The majority of Americans believe the increased focus on sexual harassment
> has made it more difficult for men to know how to interact with women
> at work.

Although women have a different physiology than you, studies prove that we are *not* an alien species. (Refer back to Chapter 4.) Don't blow the gender thing out of proportion and behave as though she's so foreign and impossible to relate to. Your female coworker will pick up on any discomfort and respond by keeping her distance, making it impossible to partner on projects and tasks. She's actually way more like you than you might realize.

Your behavior at work will have a major impact not only on your performance, but the performance of the company and the overall morale of your coworkers. By taking control of how you think, you'll be in a far better position to use all the tools we've discussed thus far. Establish trust with your coworkers with your behavior first—advocate for her, encourage her, and appreciate her teamwork. Do your best to create meaningful relationships—move away from your desk and devices, increase face time, and communicate.

Good manners and proper office etiquette cannot guarantee success on their own. The underlying reason behind your behavior is more important. *Why* are you acting the way you are? From Peter Post's *Essential Manners for Men*:

Etiquette is about being considerate and honest with others. Manners matter, because manners are really about showing respect for another person. We hold the door for a woman not because there's a rule that says we should, but because it is an act of kindness and a way to make the woman you're with feel special.[11]

In the context of modern feminism and what *GQ* magazine is promoting as "the new masculinity," a man in today's workplace must adapt to things that may seem superficial—like who pays for lunch, who goes first, and so on—but a man should not compromise who he is. To do so is to set up a false identity, and in so doing, is false to others. Thomas Jefferson said it well: "In matters of style, swim with the current; in matters of principle, stand firm like a rock."

"In matters of style, swim with the current; in matters of principle, stand firm like a rock."

What's Next for the Modern Corporate World?

How technological advances impact your workplace relationships.

Women hold 76 percent of healthcare jobs in the US, and make up 85 percent of the nursing workforce. During the pandemic, these jobs were not in jeopardy of being replaced. However, for other women, finding new avenues of work is a necessity. Hundreds of thousands of jobs traditionally held by females, such as secretaries and administrative assistants, are expected to disappear over the next few years as companies replace workers with software and other technology, according to the Bureau of Labor Statistics.[1] Technological advancements are outpacing human productivity.

The coronavirus pandemic prompted many companies to permit office workers to work from home—**telecommuting**. This is a big benefit for women since they are (usually) the primary caregiver. These employers say it can yield better access to talent and a better culture. The problem? It all hinges on whether remote workers can maintain their sense of collaboration and maintain productivity without feeling left out and isolated. As we discussed in Chapter 7, communication is your key to success. Communication becomes an even more delicate issue when employees work from home.

To tackle this challenge, a software services company, CloudBees, developed a set of "netiquette" rules.[2] They apply to both genders. "Netiquette" instructs employees to be considerate of one another, such as rotating time zones for meetings when people aren't in the same locations. Also, messaging tools like Slack can make it easier for colleagues to share nonverbal cues like high fives or a smiley-face emoji.

Morgan Wright worked for Cisco Systems when they introduced "Telepresence"—a videoconferencing system designed to link two physically separate rooms regardless of location. He recalled his excitement to me: "It changed the dynamics and intimacy of conversation. It also had an unforeseen downside. . . . It was too easy to press 'end' and walk away knowing that the other person might be hundreds or even thousands of miles away." Wright told me that technology will never be a substitute for human-to-human interaction. "We must guard against thinking real relationships can be built strictly using modern technology. They can't." How women build relationships is far different than men. It would be a mistake for men to think all relationships are built the same way.

> "We must guard against thinking real relationships can be built strictly using modern technology. They can't."

Distracted in a Digital World

According to Esther Perel, psychotherapist and work counselor:

> In this new normal, relationships inside companies take on outsize importance. Yet managers' people skills are out of practice in what is called a "dehumanized" work environment. Daily conversations with coworkers occur via email and chat, candidates interview for jobs by videotaping answers to prompts on a screen and remote employees can feel well working remotely.[3]

Quite often, companies complain that young employees seem allergic to picking up the phone and calling someone, and burn out, in the form of constant email and notifications. While the internet has dramatically increased productivity in a lot of areas at work, our individual ability to concentrate is being distracted by this digital world.

Smartphones have become a big part of our daily lives. It's like you have two different worlds—the real world and the virtual world. The impact of interruptions on your productivity in the workplace is catastrophic. On average, employees check their smartphones once every twelve minutes at work. Seventy-one percent of employees never turn their phones off. And 40 percent say they check them within five minutes of waking.[4] That's a problem!

> Seventy-one percent of employees never turn their phones off. And 40 percent say they check them within five minutes of waking.

Even social media giants like Facebook and Instagram are developing tools designed to limit usage in response to claims that excessive use of social media can have a negative impact on your mental health.[5] David Galullo is the chief executive officer of Rapt Studio, a design firm. Rapt recently created an office with slots built into the door for every employee to deposit their cell phones prior to entering so they can focus.[6]

You must be responsive and attentive when you're having a conversation with a colleague, especially a woman. As we discussed in Chapter 8, when a woman is talking to you, the most important thing you can do is listen. In a world where digital communication is becoming the preferred method to conduct business, how can employers get people to take a break from their smartphones? Write a note. Eight in ten American adults prefer a handwritten note to other forms of communication, with millennials surprisingly leading the pack at 87 percent.[7]

Belfor Property Restoration chief executive officer Sheldon Yellen handwrites birthday cards for twelve thousand employees and has for decades. A handwritten note lets an employee know that you care, he told me. "We get to serve people that have lost their homes, their businesses, and help restore their lives."

| A handwritten note lets an employee know that you care.

Yellen said his notes are a "culture builder," proving that a random act of kindness goes a long way. "One of the cheapest things you can do in life to make a difference is just by being nice."[8]

Yellen has noticed some employees collect the various cards he's written to them over the years, and he realizes that his good deed has become contagious. "They, too, pass that on to others. Culture is the most important thing for a business, and the biggest asset you've got is the great people who run the business," he told me. It's definitely the little things that make a difference.

Habits like handwritten notes and thank-you cards will differentiate you from impersonal emails and text messages. Whenever possible, it's best to embrace communication with people in person, or at least find ways to have a "personal touch" in this cold electronic age. Make small acts of kindness through efforts that show you care.

Working Remotely

A study from IBM revealed that 54 percent of adults want to work from home.[9] The coronavirus pandemic provided, among other things, a massive experiment in telecommuting. Up to half of American employees worked from home during the COVID-19 outbreak in 2020. Millions of workers worked from home with no intention of going back to the office when the economy reopened.

According to the Brookings Institution, teleworking will continue long after the pandemic.[10] One thing is certain: remote work is here to stay. This transition was set in motion with big tech companies like Facebook taking the initiative by telling employees to work remotely for the entire year. Twitter took more drastic measures and allows almost all employees to work from home.[11]

Teleworking is a very attractive arrangement for workers because it translates to a number of benefits through increased flexibility. Here are four reasons why teleworking is so appealing:

1. **Work-life balance**—From continuing education to childcare responsibilities, most professionals (mainly women) have a lot to take care of outside the workplace. A teleworking arrangement allows for employees to have flexibility.

2. **Less stress**—Anyone who has ever worked in an office environment knows it can be stressful. You have to navigate different personalities, manage office politics, and be on your best behavior, especially when your boss is around.

3. **Choice of venue**—The best office environment is no match for the local park or your favorite coffee shop.

4. **No commute**—How many hours per week do you spend getting to and from work? Those hours are essentially "lost time." Research shows that people who have longer commutes report lower levels of job satisfaction than those who do not.[12]

The pandemic changed the way some corporations do business. Global downloads of business applications, including Zoom and Slack, have risen nearly fivefold since January 2020.[13] The pandemic outbreak forced companies to heavily rely on conferencing tools because workers were not allowed to go to the office. These services range from video-conferencing apps, such as Google Meets and Cisco's WebEx, to Skype to make remote work more manageable. Here are a few:

- **Zoom:** This popular conferencing app offers an unlimited number of videotelephone and online chat services through a cloud-based peer-to-peer software platform and is used for tele-conferencing. You can enable "touch up my appearance" for a subtle video enhancement that reduces under-eye baggage and mild skin blemishes, giving you a more polished look. (Women love this!) And virtual backgrounds can hide home chaos or background clutter. It's easy to share your screen and great for highly collaborative teams, like engineers.

- **Slack:** If your colleagues use Slack, but you've resisted it, this might be the right time to get on board. Imagine a work-centric group chat that doesn't disappear. That's the basic idea, but the platform can also function as a powerful substitute for in-person meetings or even a videoconference. You can create "channels," as the company calls them, each devoted to a specific project or subject. They resemble email threads, but are easier to manage and follow because Slack's searchable archive function allows you to figure out who said what and when. *Just in case you weren't listening.*

- **Google Meets:** For better or for worse, the Google ecosystem is ubiquitous, so there's a decent chance the people you want to reach have a Gmail account required to access it for free. In its basic form, Google Meets places no limit on the duration of meetings, but attendance on free video calls is capped.

- **Cisco's WebEx:** Depending on your needs, this is a favorite for small- to midsize businesses. The tool offers a plethora of services bundled together. The rich video quality plans can be accessed across any and all devices on a dial-in number with coverage in forty-five countries. Cisco WebEx meetings are also generally smooth with good playback and very little lag.

- **Skype:** Many people have used Skype at some point, so familiarity is a plus. Throughout the pandemic, most media journalists and TV commentators, like myself, broadcasted via Skype. Skype allows you to video call multiple users at the same time, and even record your video calls if needed. You can share your screen during a video call and turn on live subtitles for increased accessibility.

A luxury retailer vice president in New York City told me, "We use Skype Business, but they are all very similar apps. You can share your screen and also use the mobile app on your phone instead of the camera on your laptop. We love it!"

Of course, some jobs simply can't be done from home, but the pandemic accelerated this trend toward telecommuting. However, there are a few high-profile companies, such as Yahoo and Reddit, who have publicly moved away from remote work. Why? Because productivity boosts aren't guaranteed, especially if an employee's performance is difficult to monitor.

Furthermore, certain employees are dependent on the culture and capabilities that a centralized office can produce. For example, "stock traders depend on the type of high-speed internet access that can't always be accessed from home," says Tina Witney, managing director at Deloitte.[14] This is the flip side of technology advancements.

The Flip Side of Technology Advancements

Walmart patented a system that takes employee monitoring to a whole new level. The retail giant listens in on their workers. Walmart calls the system, "Listening to the Frontend." It uses "sound sensors" to zero in on customers' shopping experiences. It can also monitor specific noises, like the beeps of item scanners and rustling of bags and even the conversations of workers.[15] Talk about an invasion of privacy!

Because of things like this, employees can no longer keep a secret. With advances in technology, privacy has become a privilege at work. Smartphones have become common, employees are recording work conversations without employers' knowledge or permission in preparation for discrimination, sexual harassment, and whistleblower lawsuits. Jay Holland, an attorney with Joseph Greenwald & Lake in Greenbelt, Maryland, said: "A recording of sexual harassment or a discriminatory comment can be very powerful evidence and damaging to the employer."[16]

Society no longer tolerates unacceptable behavior—try taking a donut from the morning breakfast meeting, then dropping it on the floor and putting it back to get another one. That video will show up at this year's holiday party. Guaranteed.

If you take a fancy pen from your boss's desk and tuck it into your jacket pocket, you may not think anyone saw you, but rest assured someone did. A female coworker may walk by with toilet paper stuck on her heels . . . everyone saw her. Again, no act or embarrassing moment goes unseen, thanks to the presence of cameras everywhere. This is the growing reality, like it or not.

Corporate interest in surveillance is on the rise. A survey by research firm Gartner asked 239 companies what types of technologies they are using to "track and understand the sentiment of their employees." Fifty-seven percent said they expect to monitor employee data such as movement, texts in internal messaging systems, workspace usage, and biometric monitoring.[17]

> Fifty-seven percent said they expect to monitor employee data such as movement, texts in internal messaging systems, workspace usage, and biometric monitoring.

There are numerous advantages for companies in tracking employees' work habits, movements, and even conversations. For example, UPS uses sensors in their delivery trucks to track the vehicles' usage so that maintenance can be done on an optimal schedule. The data also monitors whether drivers are wearing their seat belts and when they are opening and locking the truck doors.

The public relations manager at UPS, Dan McMackin, said vehicle sensors have helped the delivery company "avoid millions of dollars in repairs and extend fluid intervals on our fleet of more than 100,000 trucks and trailers." UPS has also used the data as a safety awareness tool, which has helped improve employee compliance with certain training protocols, he added.[18]

Elon Musk, the billionaire founder of Tesla and SpaceX, two major companies that are changing the world, came under heavy pressure for smoking marijuana during a nightly podcast interview. Following the incident, two senior-level employees resigned, and the stock tanked 11 percent. Even billionaires aren't safe.[19]

Technological advances have often put workers beneath a microscope. It doesn't matter how much money you have or how much power you may think you have, the video camera doesn't lie. Depending on the state laws, most likely, your phone calls at the office are being recorded and your work emails are being read by compliance. The Electronic Communications Privacy Act allows employers to listen in on business calls without your consent. Companies can monitor employee movement, location, and computer usage.

For example, surveillance tools are sometimes installed on employer-issued smartphones to prevent theft. Emails and phone calls using company systems and equipment can be monitored, and the content is usually archived on servers. If you're using your personal phone or tablet but also using your company's email system, employers can monitor those transmissions. Likewise, desks and offices are generally considered "employer property," meaning they can be searched.[20] These are definitely some things to keep in mind.

So, what do you do? **Answer:** Make sure you don't have something to hide and mind your manners, "mind your p's and q's." Keep your hands to yourself. Don't touch unless invited to touch. Don't steal. Don't be rude. Ditch the condescending attitude and try to be a well-mannered, politically correct professional at the office. Always beyond reproach. (*Don't put the donut back on the tray, throw it away.*) Refer back to The Secret Rules in Chapter 10.

Consequences of the 24–7 Workplace

In a twenty-four-hours-a-day, seven-days-a-week workplace—where employees, managers, and executives are expected to remain available and responsive at every moment—such ingrained corporate expectations strengthen the gender divide.

In a report, *The Design of Everyday Men*, the consulting firm Deloitte explored the organizational and cultural expectations that drive male behavior in the workplace. They connect the difficulties in achieving workplace gender equity with traditional expectations of men within many corporate cultures. And just as many women believe that they must either cut back on their work schedules or abandon their careers to take care of their children.

Why do corporations still struggle with gender equality?

Deloitte says, "Some men still feel culturally constrained to relentlessly pursue status in the workplace, thus preventing them from sharing nonwork responsibilities with their partners in a way that would allow women to more easily advance."[21]

> "Some men still feel culturally constrained to relentlessly pursue status in the workplace, thus preventing them from sharing nonwork responsibilities with their partners in a way that would allow women to more easily advance."

Many men believe they must prioritize achievement in their career above all else. This expectation means, on some level, that men are compelled to minimize involvement in their families' lives and the domestic sphere (in general) in order to maintain their status at work. Today's 24–7 workplace is the main factor holding back gender equality at executive levels.

> Individuals often prioritize work over family, personal commitments and well-being to rise to the top, and men may be more predisposed to making this trade off at the expense of their outside-of-work-commitments. Women then wind up picking up the slack on household and other nonwork responsibilities, thereby [disadvantaging] themselves by becoming unable to adhere to the "always on, always available" expectation as easily.[22]

In the pressure cooker of the modern workplace and the modern family, it's past time for both men and women to step back and examine what drives their behaviors both at work and at home. I'm not saying that there is anything wrong with being driven to achieve at work or being content at home raising children. The point I'm making is that whatever choice you're making, it should be intentional. You need to understand the trade-offs involved in every choice you make, and the costs and benefits of those choices for your family.

There is no rule that you have to be number one at work. (I once believed that was the *only* rule.) Maybe you'd actually be happier being number two or number three, number twenty-three or number 2,003. In thinking this through, you may have to dig deep, working past cultural, family, and workplace expectations to really consider what type of lifestyle you want and what type of person, husband, and father you want to be. Whatever you discover, integrating those desires into your career and your personal life will help you become a more integrated, authentic person.

Deloitte's report identifies four tendencies that constrain professional men to their jobs, at the expense of their families and to the ultimate detriment of a truly equal workplace:

- **Individualistic focus:** Men place enormous pressure on themselves to handle responsibilities on their own as individuals.

- **Fear of failure:** Men are afraid of failure, which leads them to overcompensate with hyper-competitive behavior to mask their insecurity and earn professional success.

- **Difficulty building connections:** Personal relationships and vulnerable interactions help to alleviate pressure and fear, but men have difficulty building those connections.

- **Behavior modeling:** Men look to leaders and peers in their companies to understand what behaviors are acceptable and lead to status.[23]

In today's collaborative workplace, these tendencies might get you ahead in the short term, but they aren't likely to serve you or the company you work for in the long term. Companies seek leaders, managers, and employees who can function effectively and efficiently in diverse teams. That puts the focus on building relationships, cultivating authenticity, and working collaboratively to achieve goals. It also means valuing and recognizing the contributions of everyone, not just the boss or the person with the highest status.

Employees Seek Comfort in the Office

New offices are seeking comfort and fewer distractions because employees are "distracted in a digital world." According to the *Wall Street Journal,* the latest corporate offices include employees' workspace ideas, as companies strive to retain talent. Here are a few examples: piping white noise in through the ceiling to prevent distractions; a corridor with sliding floor-to-ceiling windows that open to nature; nearby public hiking and biking trails that intersect with the office; and meeting rooms that include a "no screen" policy (cell phones should be left at the door).[24]

Even the little details, like the office temperature, can have a big impact on women's performance. Researchers suggest that mixed-gender offices should increase their temperatures. Why? According to Tom Chang of USC's Marshall School of Business, "What we found is it's not just whether you feel comfortable or not, but that your performance on things that matter—in math and verbal dimensions, and how hard you try—is affected by temperature."[25] This means that there may be an ideal temperature where the entire team performs better.

According to Andrews Sykes Group, 2 percent of the average working day is wasted over climate control issues, costing the economy $13 billion annually.[26] Furthermore, women feel colder than men do at the same air temperature. One study from the Eindhoven University of Technology found that men prefer rooms at seventy-two degrees Fahrenheit, while women prefer seventy-seven degrees Fahrenheit. Body size and fat-to-muscle ratios are largely to blame.[27]

> Men prefer rooms at seventy-two degrees Fahrenheit, while women prefer
> seventy-seven degrees Fahrenheit. Body size and fat-to-muscle ratios are
> largely to blame.

Quartz's Gwynn Guilford explained that the discrepancy dates back to the 1960s and '70s, when scientists and regulators set workplace indoor climate standards based on the metabolic rate of a forty-year-old man weighing 154 pounds. Times have changed.

As we discussed in Chapter 5, McDonald's is adapting to these gender needs. They developed an app that lets employees adjust the temperature in their workspace and aims to comfort women in the inclusive modern workplace.

Expedia Group has a main corporate campus in Seattle, Washington. Their research indicated that employees—both men and women—want more natural light and views. So, the company incorporated a grass-roofed conference space that includes a wall of windows overlooking the water.[28] (*I wonder what they do when it rains.*)

And then there's Walmart, which has a 350-acre corporate campus designed to house as many as 17,000 employees. The campus features walking paths surrounding 15 acres of lakes, a gym, and an on-site childcare center for your kids.[29] Talk about adapting to a woman's needs.

Conclusion

The chief economist of Moody's, Mark Zandi, said, "Women are now the majority of the workforce and there is no looking back!" He added: "Women are going to increasingly dominate the labor market."[1] This continued growth in employment for women parallels the economic shift away from so-called traditional, male-dominated jobs in sectors such as manufacturing toward a service-based business model. Betsey Stevenson, a professor at the University of Michigan, said, "Women are going into the types of occupations where jobs are growing more rapidly, so this trend isn't going to reverse."[2]

Importance of Recognition

In a report, "The Future of Work Is Human," WorkHuman, a social recognition and performance management platform, found a strong correlation between the frequency of recognition at work and lower stress levels.[3] On a fundamental level, we all long to be seen and recognized for who we are and what we're accomplishing, as we discussed in Chapter 7. And since we spend so much of our time at work, it's only natural that we seek validation at the office.

> There's a strong correlation between the frequency of recognition at work and lower stress levels.

Appreciation is a great way to break down barriers and build relationships with women. Not only does it benefit your team and your coworkers, it will decrease any sense of isolation you may feel and build important social bonds with your coworkers. In our "me first" culture, it's easy to think that we should get all the credit. However, it's an amazing feeling to generously share credit and to give credit and appreciation where credit and appreciation are due. Most managers and even executives are actually bad at this. If you want to climb the corporate ladder, get into the habit of copying a coworker's manager in thank-you emails and giving others credit in meetings.

When asked what one aspect of their workplace they would change, employees who responded to a WorkHuman survey reported that they seek more appreciation for the efforts they put in at work. In a similar fashion, they stated that there is one thing that they'd like their managers to do more often—show more appreciation for the hard work they do. The future is bright for corporations that leverage human applications to build up gratitude, empower employees to drive their own development, and take an unapologetic stance toward greater equity for all.

> The future is bright for corporations that leverage human applications to build up gratitude, empower employees to drive their own development, and take an unapologetic stance toward greater equity for all.

Inclusion Best Practices

On a personal and organizational level, success or failure in adapting to gender inclusion increasingly defines brands, reputations, and legacies. Throughout this book, you've read about the adverse consequences that companies and individuals experienced in the wake of gender inclusion blunders. To put it bluntly, no one wants to be the next Harvey Weinstein or Uber. **The Bottom Line:** You can either graciously get on the inclusion bandwagon, or you can get dragged on it.

With that in mind, here are my five best practices for building an inclusive workplace in your corner of the universe:

1. **Banish fear:** Fear of working with women can poison your workplace and foster division. Challenging beliefs that lead to exclusion and discrimination can be difficult, as managers and employees may react negatively. A focus on creating shared goals around gender inclusion and celebrating the benefits can counteract the natural fears that change brings.

2. **Create belonging:** Humans are wired to connect and want to belong. Corporations, employees, managers, and leaders that create a sense of belonging among everyone are far more likely to succeed in creating and maintaining gender inclusion. Affirming and recognizing the accomplishments of everyone also goes a long way to sustaining a sense of belonging.

3. **Model inclusion:** Enforcing policies from above doesn't work. Men, especially, need to know what inclusion looks like from their leaders, managers, and colleagues. If you're trying to create a more family-friendly, inclusive workplace by promoting paternity leave, for example, it's not enough to put a policy in the employee handbook. Instead, walk the walk. Be like Mark Zuckerberg of Facebook, who took several months of paternity leave after his second daughter was born.[4]

4. **Foster empathy:** Empathy opposes gender discrimination and exclusion. Encourage your direct reports, teams, and colleagues to remember and share times that they were excluded. In fact, think of some exclusion experiences yourself if you're tempted to get closed-minded about inclusion. Everyone can empathize with exclusion that doesn't seem fair. Maybe you can identify with a female colleague who was passed over for promotion by recalling your experience getting rejected from the college of your dreams.

5. **Enforce consequences:** Finally, don't look the other way if you see gender discrimination, or harassment; immediately report the incident to human resources. It's also (sometimes) okay to have a conversation with the victim, but use your best judgment. The only way gender discrimination and harassment will end in your workplace is if everyone works together to end it.

Thriving in the Workplace of the Future

As America becomes more diverse, the workplace follows. That means diversity and inclusion will no longer be buzzwords, nor will policies be mandated from above—they will be a necessary part of a successful day-to-day business strategy. Why? Because the American population is expected to get older and more racially diverse during the next decade. Although this book focuses solely on the gender aspect of inclusion, diversity trends will accelerate in the 2040s. By 2045, non-Hispanic white people will be a minority.[5] In New York, this is already the case.[6]

It's finally time to embrace a more diverse workplace. Gwen Moran writes in *Fast Company* that these coming demographic changes will by necessity force corporations to become more adaptable: "As a shortage of knowledge workers forces organizations to cast a wider net for talent, tapping new regions or underutilized demographic segments, cultures will need to focus on inclusion to create harmonious, productive, work environments."[7]

> "As a shortage of knowledge workers forces organizations to cast a wider net for talent, tapping new regions or underutilized demographic segments, cultures will need to focus on inclusion to create harmonious, productive, work environments."

Rapidly evolving technology means that communication platforms will change, heightening the importance of communication skills across text, audio, video, and virtual reality, Moran adds. McKinsey emphasized how the coming seismic changes in technology will alter the workplace of the future in its report *Skill Shift: Automation and the Future of the Workforce.*

For highly skilled workers, the coming changes are less about losing a job to automation than the ways that companies will adapt in the future. Cross-functional and team-based work will predominate. Leaders, managers, and employees will constantly need to update their skills, as companies redeploy workforces to meet changing demands.[8]

As I've noted, the inclusive workforce requires the development of social and emotional skills. These are also skills that robots aren't likely to master anytime soon. McKinsey notes: "Workers of the future will spend considerably more time deploying social and emotional skills than they do today."[9] While some of these social and emotional skills are innate, such as empathy, they can be honed, and, to some extent, taught more easily than technological skills—for example, advanced communication.

> "Workers of the future will spend considerably more time deploying social and emotional skills than they do today."

This is one of the biggest challenges all of us—both men and women—face. And it's not going to get easier. To not just survive, but flourish in the workplace of the future, you'll need to constantly upgrade and fine-tune your communications skills. That's because it takes even more skill to communicate with people who have different backgrounds and experiences. To do that successfully, you'll need an open mind, generosity of spirit, and a willingness to learn, and keep learning.

If you think about it, just about every facet of every job hinges on communication, as we discussed in Chapter 7. To complete tasks successfully, you have to work with women. To deal with women successfully, you have to communicate diplomatically. Humility is important too.

The well-known Dunning-Kruger effect demonstrates that the less a person actually knows about a subject, the more confident and assertive they tend to be about that subject. Put another way, certainty about the world is inversely related to wisdom. That said, the perception of confidence in executives is vital. Know when to strike a confident tone in the office, but also learn to read irrational exuberance in others.

Most people can be easily swayed by others who speak with conviction, but have done very little research. "Experts" often get into the opposite trap by falling into the arrogance of their own credentials and egos. The tightrope walk between humility and confidence is resolved by realizing they are not opposite forces—the best leaders marry the two traits into one package.

> The tightrope walk between humility and confidence is resolved by realizing they are not opposite forces—the best leaders marry the two traits into one package.

Learn how to think and speak probabilistically about outcomes and scenarios. Doubt and question your own conclusions. Encourage others to use their experience to challenge your hypothesis. Think critically and leverage your full team. Learn to use counterfactuals. Realize there are always unforeseen risks, and the biggest risk is always the one you haven't considered.

We all can learn something from each and every person we encounter—male or female. The best way to adapt and thrive in the diverse and inclusive workplace of today and tomorrow is to treat everyone with respect, practice kindness, and share your appreciation.

This book champions how far we've come, in terms of workplace gender equality. I agree that more can be done, but constant criticism and blame do not pave the way to achieve parity. You can shed light on gender issues in the workplace in a way that can positively impact corporate culture without conflict and drama. It just takes an open mind and mutual respect for both genders. Genuine collaboration leads to positive change, in contrast to defensive-oriented diversity and inclusion policies.

> Genuine collaboration leads to positive change, in contrast to defensive-oriented diversity and inclusion policies.

I mean, really, who wants to attend another diversity and inclusion training course? When employees, managers, and leaders share responsibility for creating and sustaining an inclusive workplace, those values are more likely to permeate the company.

An African proverb notes that it takes a village to raise a child. At work, it takes a village to create inclusion—and that means each and every one of us. As Gallup notes, an inclusive workplace culture involves everyone treating everyone else with respect: "Building an inclusive culture is the shared responsibility of employees, managers and organizational leaders. It takes intention at every level to sustain an inclusive workplace."[10]

> "Building an inclusive culture is the shared responsibility of employees, managers and organizational leaders. It takes intention at every level to sustain an inclusive workplace."

RECAP

The secret rules to successfully work with women.

D on't overwhelm yourself with The Secret Rules outlined in the guide. Merely consider thinking a little differently about your interactions with women in the workplace. Think about which of these skills can help you most. Some of these may seem obvious, but the point is—they are actually uncommon. Maybe you are already one step ahead of these guidelines. My advice to those men who already "get it" is to use these strategies to sharpen your skill set. It's not just about riding in on a white horse to protect women like Bud White in the movie *L.A. Confidential.* The smart thing is knowing when to back off and when to go to HR.

For most, a little effort can save your job and get you the promotion you've always dreamed of. By keeping a few concepts in mind, you will become the best version of you in this new normal—the inclusive twenty-first century workplace.

The Secret Rules

#1 Keep communication professional
#2 Respect personal space
#3 Dine out in groups
#4 Give neutral compliments
#5 Make proper introductions
#6 Keep the door open during office meetings

#7   Think before you speak

#8   Dress for success

#9   Hold the door open for everyone

#10 Give a consistent handshake

#11 Listen actively

#12 Treat everyone with respect

#13 Find commonalities

EPILOGUE

Wearing my cultural critic hat.

Too often, mainstream feminism becomes obsessed with victimhood. The rhetoric is concerned with what women can't do as opposed to what we can. The very people who supposedly champion the ability of women to break through limitations spend much of their time promoting a victimhood narrative that weakens the image of professional working women while unnecessarily characterizing men as victimizers, a slur that is increasingly unfair.

The emphasis in society and politics is more commonly on our differences—what separates us from one another, not what unites us. We may not be there yet, but if the goal of feminism is equality of opportunity, at some point we have to find a more cooperative model. We should never compromise or be less intolerant of sexism, but society will never change if men are presumed guilty before being proven innocent.

I am lucky. I've had a lot of supportive men throughout my life and career, starting with my dad. He encouraged me to have ambition, and he didn't treat me any differently than my older brother. Being a woman was neither a limitation nor a feature. Ever. It was never discussed, period. A victim mentality—blaming "the system" for one's own personal failures—was not allowed in our house.

In *Lean In: Women, Work, and the Will to Lead,* Facebook's chief operating officer, Sheryl Sandberg, wrote: "The gender stereotypes introduced in childhood are reinforced throughout our lives and become self-fulfilling prophesies. Most leadership positions are held by men, so women don't expect to achieve them, and that becomes one of the reasons they don't."

> "The gender stereotypes introduced in childhood are reinforced throughout our lives and become self-fulfilling prophesies. Most leadership positions are held by men, so women don't expect to achieve them, and that becomes one of the reasons they don't."

Or maybe it's because they don't want them. Why? Well, I could think of a few reasons: they like their current job, they have no interest in managing people, or they don't want to work more than forty hours a week. Or maybe it's because women just don't have the time. Personally, I never figured out the whole work/life balance thing.

Spending more time with family is a factor for some women to take a step down.[1] In a CNBC article, former PepsiCo chief executive officer Indra Nooyi said: "I've been blessed with an amazing career, but if I'm being honest, there have been moments I wish I'd spent more time with my children and family."

> "I've been blessed with an amazing career, but if I'm being honest, there have been moments I wish I'd spent more time with my children and family."

Or maybe it's because many women are simply smart enough to know there's more to life than running things in a corporate world.

Sexual Suicide

George Gilder authored two minor sociological classics in the early 1970s: *Naked Nomads* and *Sexual Suicide.* Gilder looked at how young men are socialized into family life and the role women play in convincing young men to surrender freedom and accept responsibility in its place. So here you are. You're working in a corporate culture that has changed, and changed rapidly, presenting new challenges.

If you listen to any new country, rock, or rap tune, and if the singer is male, the song is likely to be about living it up—meeting a girl, having a party, driving fast cars, and so on. Seldom does one encounter a star who wrote lyrics about settling down and the responsibilities of family life.

Love him or hate him, rapper Kanye West hit the nail on the head when he summed up youth culture: "We want to spend all our money on luxury, as opposed to going and buying some land (investing). . . . The culture has you focused so much on . . . pulling up in a foreign (sports car) and rapping about things that could get you locked up . . . I have turned my back on the idea of a victimization mentality."

"We're brainwashed," Kanye said in an interview.[2] That's the dilemma Gilder wrote about. A young man's freedom and society's need for him to surrender that freedom for the responsibilities of family life are at odds.

Family First

In the wake of the 2008 financial crisis, more men lost their jobs than women. In turn, this forced more women into the workforce, leaving the childcare responsibilities on the newly unemployed men. As the economy improved, gender equality reverted back to the pre-crisis division of labor until COVID-19 emerged. Once again, women became the primary caretakers of the family. The *New York Times* said it best: "In the Covid-19 economy, you can have a kid or a job. You can't have both." This shifting change in gender dynamics continued throughout the crisis.

A *National Review* essay called "Leaning Out" by Patrick T. Brown addresses this. Brown argues that public policy should make it easier for one parent to stay home, like the mother. "Our political class studiously contemplates how to help women 'have it all.' What if we made it easier for moms to lean out?"[3]

> "Our political class studiously contemplates how to help women 'have it all.'
> What if we made it easier for moms to lean out?"

Wall Street types seem to believe that it's best for a family to have two working parents, but surveys of the general population tell a much different story. The Brookings Institution reported that the stalling rate of women's labor-force participation is a threat to "economic progress." In another report, the OECD economists cited the country's high proportion of stay-at-home moms as the "greatest untapped potential" for the country's workforce.

Left unexamined, Brown said, is the premise that the pursuit of economic growth is a greater social good than supporting moms who want to stay home with their children, especially in the early years of the child's life. This argument supports the book's opposing idea of gender equality in the workplace—men will continue to excel in their careers (maintaining a male-dominant corporate culture) while women focus on responsibilities at home. But what's wrong with that?

In my early thirties, I was married and had just had a baby. I found myself physically and mentally exhausted when I came home from work. I didn't work hard because I had to; I worked hard because I was addicted to winning. I was competitive.

In ESPN's Chicago Bulls documentary *The Last Dance*, Michael Jordan revealed to us just how much "winning" meant to him. Tearing up, Jordan exclaimed, "Winning has a price. Leadership has a price."[4] As a result of my competitiveness, I sacrificed the early years of my marriage for tangible awards and financial gain. It's not that I didn't love my family, it's that I was overwhelmed.

The Bottom Line: If women put more hours into household activities than men, this greatly disadvantages women in the workplace, and vice versa. If this is the case, it may be unrealistic to expect gender equality in the workplace. While I don't have a solution to this problem (I will leave that to public policy and legal experts to solve), I do think it's worth our attention, so we deal with these issues in a way that challenges the status quo.

ACKNOWLEDGMENTS

First and foremost, thank you to HarperCollins Leadership. You provide people with the tools and insights to thrive in their careers. My acquisitions editor, Sara Kendricks, embraced this idea and gave me room to explore it. Senior Marketing Manager Becky Powell, Aryn Van Dyke, and Art Director Ron Huizinga, who designed and created the cover, helped the book come alive.

Thanks to Managing Editor Jeff Farr, Beth Metrick, and Zoe Kaplan at Neuwirth & Associates, who designed and copyedited *The Man's Guide to Corporate Culture*. It's absolutely perfect. Your attention to detail is remarkable.

Thanks to Amy Buttell at Kevin Anderson & Associates for your in-depth research and ideas. You clearly and concisely transformed my anecdotal stories. Your business acumen and overall knowledge of the financial industry is unparalleled.

Peggy Mercer's encouraging coaching kept me on track. You pushed me through mental roadblocks along the way. Your passion for writing made what was often a gruesome process fun.

I am forever grateful to the business leaders, financial advisors, and corporate executives who trusted me to interview them anonymously. The book is a complete source because of your personal stories and experiences.

Thanks to Kevin Anderson & Associates, Brendan Hughes, and Olin Wethington for your meticulous revisions and suggestions.

Professor Lloyd Conway enthusiastically provided historical context and economic background. You are an inspirational teacher.

Thanks to James (Jim) Trusty at Ifrah Law, Anaeli Petisco-Rojas at Chartwell Law, and Jennifer Zumarraga at Sass Law Firm for their expertise.

Thank you, SunAmerica. The vast experience I gained in the financial services industry could never be learned in a classroom setting.

Dave Gard, Jim Nichols, and Peter Harbeck at AIG allowed me to pursue other media endeavors while being employed. I am forever grateful for the opportunities you provided me.

Thanks to Fox Business, Fox News, and Newsmax TV for promoting the book.

My husband, Danny, and our sweet daughter, Samantha, allowed me hundreds of endless nights to complete this project. You were my partners along the way, whether you wanted to be or not. I love you.

My brother, Brendan Hughes, reminded me what is important. My parents, Kevin and Karen Hughes, encouraged me to strive for success. You always believed in me, Mom and Dad.

Last but not least, thanks to YOU for supporting and reading *The Man's Guide to Corporate Culture.* I sincerely hope it leads to a more peaceful and joyous life in the workplace.

ENDNOTES

Introduction

1. Adam Baidawi, "Henry Cavill on His Best Life Lessons: 'Your Head Can Be Messed with, but It's Down to Me to Deal with That,'" *GQ Australia*, July 10, 2018, https://www.gq.com.au/entertainment/celebrity/henry-cavill/image-gallery/.

Chapter 1

1. Amara Omeokwe, "Women Overtake Men as Majority of U.S. Workforce," *Wall Street Journal*, January 10, 2020, https://www.wsj.com/articles/women-overtake-men-as-majority-of-u-s-workforce-11578670615?

2. Christine Lagarde and Jonathan D. Ostry, "When more women join the workforce, everyone benefits. Here's why," *World Economic Forum*, December 4, 2018, https://www.weforum.org/agenda/2018/12/economic-gains-from-gender-inclusion-even-greater-than-you-thought/.

3. Lagarde and Ostry, "When more women join the workforce."

4. Elizabeth Segran, "The unbearable maleness of Victoria's Secret could be its undoing," *Fast Company*, September 13, 2019, https://www.fastcompany.com/90403167/victorias-secret-could-be-undone-by-unbearable-maleness.

5. Paul Ausick, "A Record Number of Women Become CEOs in 2019, but Is That Good Enough?" *24/7 Wall St.*, January 15, 2020, https://247wallst.com/jobs/2020/01/15/a-record-number-of-women-become-ceos-in-2019-but-is-that-good-enough/.

6. *Forbes* profile, Marillyn Hewson, *Forbes*, https://www.forbes.com/profile/marillyn-hewson/#6fe1e963736a.

7. *Forbes* profile, Meg Whitman, *Forbes*, https://www.forbes.com/profile/meg-whitman/#4cd2d68363cc.

8. Mary T. Barra biography, General Motors, https://www.gm.com/our-company/leadership/corporate-officers.html.

9. Jack Kelly, "Women Now Hold More Jobs Than Men in the U.S. Workforce," *Forbes*, January 13, 2020, https://www.forbes.com/sites/jackkelly/2020/01/13/women-now-hold-more-jobs-than-men/.

10. "Men continue to pull back from interacting with women in the wake of #MeToo," SurveyMonkey.com, May 17, 2019, https://www.surveymonkey.com/newsroom/men-continue-to-pull-back-in-wake-of-metoo/.

11. Heather Haddon, "McDonald's Fires CEO Steve Easterbrook over Relationship with Employee," *Wall Street Journal*, November 4, 2019, https://www.wsj.com /articles/mcdonalds-fires-ceo-steve-easterbrook-over-relationship-with -employee-11572816660.

12. Cathy Bussewitz and Dee-Ann Durbin, "McDonald's CEO Pushed Out after Relationship with Employee," AP News, November 3, 2019, https://apnews.com /7b8aa56cb9194edc8802093085f4c254.

13. Mike Isaac, "Inside Uber's Aggressive, Unrestrained Workplace Culture," *New York Times*, February 22, 2017, https://www.nytimes.com/2017/02/22/technology /uber-workplace-culture.html.

14. Nicholas Pearce, "Here's Where Travis Kalanick Really Went Wrong with Uber's Harassment Claims," *Fortune*, February 23, 2017, https://fortune.com/2017/02/23 /uber-travis-kalanick-harassment/.

15. Jack Kelly, "Four CEOs Were Dethroned Just This Week: The Days of the Powerful Untouchable CEO May Be Over," *Forbes*, September 26, 2019, https://www.forbes .com/sites/jackkelly/2019/09/26/four-ceos-were-dethroned-just-this-week-the -days-of-the-powerful-untouchable-ceo-may-be-over/.

16. Sarah Nassauer and Dana Mattioli, "Best Buy Opens Probe into CEO's Personal Conduct," *Wall Street Journal*, January 17, 2020, https://www.wsj.com/articles/best |-buy-opens-probe-into-ceo-s-personal-conduct-11579294620.

17. Ingrid Jacques, "Jacques: Women Don't Get Free Pass from #MeToo," *Detroit News*, November 7, 2019, https://www.detroitnews.com/story/opinion/columnists /ingrid-jacques/2019/11/07/jacques-women-dont-get-free-pass-metoo /2517265001/.

18. Jacques, "Jacques."

Chapter 2

1. "Meritor Savings Bank, FSB v. Vinson," Oyez. Accessed May 24, 2020, https://www .oyez.org/cases/1985/84-1979.

2. "Meritor Savings Bank."

3. Stuart Taylor Jr., "Sex Harassment on Job Is Illegal," *New York Times*, June 20, 1986, https://www.nytimes.com/1986/06/20/us/sex-harassment-on-job-is-illegal .html. Accessed September 8, 2019.

4. Paulina Deda, "Cleveland Cavaliers' Tristan Thompson Ejected after Slapping Butt of Memphis Grizzlies' Jae Crowder," Fox News, January 18, 2020, https://www .foxnews.com/sports/cleveland-cavaliers-tristan-thompson-butt-slap-jae-crowder.

5. US Equal Employment Opportunity Commission, "Sexual Harassment," https:// www.eeoc.gov/laws/types/sexual_harassment.cfm. Accessed August 8, 2019.

6. Sachi Barreiro, "What Kinds of Behavior Are Considered Sexual Harassment?" Nolo.com, https://www.nolo.com/legal-encyclopedia/what-kinds-of-behaviors -are-considered-sexual-harassment.html. Accessed September 11, 2019.

7. Jack Kelly, "Four CEOs Were Dethroned Just This Week: The Days of the Powerful, Untouchable CEO May Be Over," *Forbes*, September 26, 2019, https://www.forbes .com/sites/jackkelly/2019/09/26/four-ceos-were-dethroned-just-this-week -the-days-of-the-powerful-untouchable-ceo-may-be-over/.

Chapter 3

1. Shelley J. Correll and Caroline Simard, "Research: Vague Feedback Is Holding Women Back," *Harvard Business Review*, April 29, 2016, https://hbr.org/2016/04 /research-vague-feedback-is-holding-women-back.

2. Michael Allison Chandler, "Men Account for Nearly 1 in 5 Complaints of Workplace Sexual Harassment with the EEOC," *Washington Post*, April 8, 2018, https://www.washingtonpost.com/local/social-issues/men-account-for-nearly-1-in-5-complaints-of-workplace-sexual-harassment-with-the-eeoc/2018/04/08/4f7a2572-3372-11e8-94fa-32d48460b955_story.html. Accessed September 11, 2019.

3. Kathy Gurchiek, "EEOC Drops Hammer on Workplace Harassment," Society for Human Resource Management, August 10, 2018, https://www.shrm.org/resources-andtools/hr-topics/employee-relations/pages/eeoc-drops-hammer-on-workplace-harassment.aspx.

4. The name, location, and job have been altered. All information provided on the case is readily available in publicly filed federal court documents. No sensitive information has been disclosed.

5. Dave Philips, "Six Men Tell Their Stories of Sexual Assault in the Military," *New York Times*, September 10, 2019, https://www.nytimes.com/interactive/2019/09/10/us/men-military-sexual-assault.html. Accessed September 11, 2019.

6. "After a year of #MeToo, American opinion has shifted against victims," *Economist*, October 15, 2018, https://www.economist.com/graphic-detail/2018/10/15/after-a-year-of-metoo-american-opinion-has-shifted-against-victims. Accessed September 11, 2019.

7. "After a year of #MeToo."

8. Vivia Chen, "#MeToo Backlash Is Not Going Away," Law.com, September 5, 2019, https://www.law.com/americanlawyer/2019/09/05/metoo-backlash-is-not-going-away/?slreturn=20200020202906.

9. David Gelles and Natalie Kitroeff, "Boeing Fires C.E.O. Dennis Muilenburg," *New York Times*, December 23, 2019, https://www.nytimes.com/2019/12/23/business/Boeing-ceo-muilenburg.html.

10. "The Best Lessons from 'Art of War,' a Book Evan Spiegel Bought Snapchat Employees When He Felt Threatened by Facebook," *Business Insider*, March 23, 2015, https://www.businessinsider.com/best-lessons-and-summary-of-the-art-of-war-by-sun-tzu-2015-3#on-tactics-plan-ahead-dont-make-it-up-as-you-go-8.

11. "Bud Fox Quotes Sun Tzu to Gordon Gekko," *Wall Street* (1987), clip from the movie, https://www.youtube.com/ watch?v=vivMOshFrP8.

12. "The Best Lessons from 'Art of War,' a Book Evan Spiegel Bought Snapchat Employees When He Felt Threatened by Facebook."

13. Hilary Wething, "Job Growth in the Great Recession Has Not Been Equal between Men and Women," *Working Economics Blog*, August 26, 2014, Economic Policy Institute, https://www.epi.org/blog/job-growth-great-recession-equal-men-women/.

14. Richard Vedder, "The Collegiate War against Men," *Forbes*, January 2, 2020, https://www.forbes.com/sites/richardvedder/2020/01/02the-collegiate-war-against-men/.

15. Wething, "Job Growth."

16. Vedder, "The Collegiate War."

17. Vedder, "The Collegiate War."

18. Julie Shaw, "Why Are We Not Outraged That Prisons Are Filled with Men?" *Psychology Today*, February 20, 2019, https://www.psychologytoday.com/us/blog/making-evil/201902/why-are-we-not-outraged-prisons-are-filled-men.

19. Shaw, "Why Are We Not Outraged."

20. "Data Visualization: Gender and Individual Homelessness," July 9, 2019, National Alliance to End Homelessness, https://endhomelessness.org/resource/data-visualization-gender-disparities-in-homelessness/.

Chapter 4

1. Bruce Goldman, "Two Minds: The Cognitive Differences between Men and Women," Stanford Medicine, Spring 2017, https://stanmed.stanford.edu/2017 spring/how-mens-and-womens-brains-are-different.html.
2. Goldman, "Two Minds."
3. Goldman, "Two Minds."
4. Shaunti Feldhahn, *The Male Factor: The Unwritten Rules, Misperceptions, and Secret Beliefs of Men in the Workplace* (New York: Currency, 2009), p. 252.
5. Feldhahn, *The Male Factor.*
6. W. Brad Johnson and David Smith, *Athena Rising: How and Why Men Should Mentor Women* (New York: Bibliomotion, 2016), p. 35.
7. Feldhahn, *The Male Factor*, p. 250.
8. Goldman, "Two Minds," Stanford Medicine, https://stanmed.stanford.edu/2017 spring/how-mens-and-womens-brains-are-different.html.
9. Goldman, "Two Minds."
10. Matilda Ruff, "Can You Really Say That at Work?" *Daily Mail,* June 6, 2019, https://www.dailymail.co.uk/femail/article-7114123/The-used-phrases-inappropriate -replace-with.html.
11. Amira Elsayed, "6 Differences between Male & Female Body Language," *Identity*, March 27, 2018, https://identity-mag.com/6-differences-between-male-female-body -language/.
12. Elsayed, "6 Differences."
13. Elsayed, "6 Differences."
14. Feldhahn, *The Male Factor*, p. 251.
15. Carol Kinsey Goman, "Is Your Communication Style Dictated by Your Gender?" *Forbes*, March 31, 2016, https://www.forbes.com/sites/carolkinseygoman/2016/03 /31/is-your-communication-style-dictated-by-your-gender/.
16. "Gender Differences in Communication Styles," Point Park University Online, December 12, 2017, https://online.pointpark.edu/public-relations-and-advertising /gender-differences-communication-styles/.
17. Chip Cutter and Rachel Feintzeig, "Office of the Future: More Perks, Less Personal Space," *Wall Street Journal*, November 23, 2019, https://www.wsj.com/articles/the -new-office-comes-designed-to-please-11574510402.

Chapter 5

1. Dale Carnegie, *How to Win Friends and Influence People* (New York: Simon and Schuster, 1981).
2. Carnegie, *How to Win Friends.*
3. Steve Hargreaves, "The Richest Americans in History," CNN, June 2, 2014, https://money.cnn.com/gallery/luxury/2014/06/01/richest-americans-in-history/index .html.
4. Craig Valentine, Mitch Meyerson, Patricia Fripp, *World Class Speaking* (New York: Morgan James Publishing, 2009), p. 68.
5. Liz Ryan, "Ten Things Never, Ever to Say at Work," *Forbes*, January 13, 2018, https://www.forbes.com/sites/lizryan/2018/01/13/ten-things-never-ever-to-say -at-work/.
6. Elizabeth Gravier, "7,000 Dogs Visit Amazon for National Take Your Dog to Work Day—but It's Just Another Day at the Office," CNBC, June 21, 2019, https://www .cnbc.com/2019/06/21/thousands-of-dogs-visit-amazons-campus-for-take -your-dog-to-work-day.html.

7. Taylor Soper, "Amazon Ranks No. 1 as Most Dog-Friendly Company in America; Trupanion at No. 3," GeekWire, June 12, 2019, https://www.geekwire.com/2019/amazon-ranks-no-1-dog-friendly-company-america-trupanion-no-3/.

8. Tom Scheve, "How Many Muscles Does It Take to Smile," How Stuff Works, https://science.howstuffworks.com/life/inside-the-mind/emotions/muscles-smile.htm.

9. Nicole Spector, "Smiling Can Trick Your Brain into Happiness—and Improve Your Health," NBC News, November 28, 2017, https://www.nbcnews.com/better/health/smiling-can-trick-your-brain-happiness-boost-your-health-ncna822591.

10. Spector, "Smiling Can Trick Your Brain."

11. David Winograd, "10 Things Super Successful People Do During Lunch," Huffpost, November 5, 2013, https://www.huffpost.com/entry/successful-people-lunch_n_4102043.

12. Francesca Fontana, "Why Women Don't Get the Feedback They Need," *Wall Street Journal*, October 12, 2019, https://www.wsj.com/articles/the-reasons-women-dont-get-the-feedback-they-need-11570872601#:~:text=Women.

13. Jane Burnett, "Almost 100% of Women Say This Is the Most Uncomfortable Work Situation," The Ladders, July 6, 2018, https://www.theladders.com/career-advice/almost-100-of-women-say-this-is-the-most-uncomfortable-work-situation.

Chapter 6

1. Billy Arcement, "What Employees Want in an Ideal Boss," The Business Journals, August 19, 2019, https://www.bizjournals.com/bizjournals/how-to/human-resources/2019/08/what-employees-want-in-an-ideal-boss.html.

2. Lyn Reese, "Female Fury in the Forum," Classroom Lesson Series, Women in World History, http://www.womeninworldhistory.com/lesson10.html. Accessed September 11, 2019.

3. Katharine K. Zarrella, "The Most Powerful Women in Business Wear Dresses, Not Suits," *Wall Street Journal*, August 29. 2019, https://www.wsj.com/articles/the-most-powerful-women-in-business-wear-dresses-not-suits-11567106879.

4. Jena McGregor, "After Years of 'Glacial' Change, Women Now Hold More Than 1 in 4 Corporate Board Seats," *Washington Post*, July 17, 2019, https://www.washingtonpost.com/business/2019/07/17/after-years-glacial-change-women-now-hold-more-than-corporate-board-seats. Accessed September 11, 2019.

5. Drew DeSilver, "A Record Number of Women Will Be Serving in the New Congress," Pew Research Center, December 18, 2018, https://www.pewresearch.org/fact-tank/2018/12/18/record-number-women-in-congress. Accessed September 11, 2018.

6. Shana Lebowitz, "11 Simple Ways to Make Your Boss Love You and Help Your Work Stand Out," *Business Insider*, January 6, 2020, https://www.businessinsider.com/how-to-make-your-boss-love-you-2016-4.

Chapter 7

1. Sophia Bendit, "How to Compliment a Woman without Making It Weird," *GQ*, March 28, 2018, https://www.gq.com/story/ne-me-creep-pas.

2. John Gray, *Men Are from Mars, Women Are from Venus* (New York: HarperCollins Interactive, 1995), p, 29.

3. Nicole Lyn Pesce, "Workers need to practice safe texts—or risk getting fired," MarketWatch, September 14, 2018, https://www.marketwatch.com/storyworkers-need-to-practice-safe-texts—or-risk-getting-fired-2018-09-14.

4. Pesce, "Workers need to practice safe texts."

5. Jacquelyn Smith, "10 Reasons Why Humor Is a Key to Success at Work," *Forbes*, May 3, 2013, https://www.forbes.com/sites/jacquelynsmith/2013/05/03/10-reasons -why-humor-is-a-key-to-success-at-work/.

6. Jonathan Evens, Jerel Slaughter, Aleksander Ellis, and Jessi Rivin, "Making Jokes during a Presentation Helps Men but Hurts Women," *Harvard Business Review*, March 11, 2019, https://hbr.org/2019/03/making-jokes-during-a-presentation-helps -men-but-hurts-women.

7. Liesl Nielsen, "CEO at tech conference cause controversy, attendees say," KSL.com, February 4, 2019, https://www.ksl.com/article/46483805/sexist-comments -from-utah-ceo-at-tech-conference-cause-controversy-attendees-say.

8. Julie Bort, "Microsoft CEO Satya Nadella Told a Cute Joke about What It's Really Like to Work with Bill Gates," Market Insider, July 17, 2019, https://markets .businessinsider.com/news/stocks/satya-nadella-bill-gates-hyperscale-database -2019-7-1028362142.

Chapter 8

1. Chip Cutter, "The Best-Managed Companies of 2019—How They Got That Way," *Wall Street Journal*, November 22, 2019, https://www.wsj.com/articles/the-best -managed-companies-of-2019and-how-they-got-that-way-11574437229.

2. Jennifer Prendki, "The Pyramid of Needs of Professional Women," LinkedIn.com, December 16, 2017, https://www.linkedin.com/pulse/pyramid-needs-professional -women-jennifer-prendki/.

3. Nichi Hodgson, "Why Do Women Talk So Much? You Asked Google—Here's the Answer," *Guardian*, https://www.theguardian.com/commentisfree/2018/feb /14/why-do-women-talk-so-much-google-autocomplete.

4. "Gender Differences in Communication Styles," Point Park University Online, December 12, 2017, https://online.pointpark.edu/public-relations-and-advertising /gender-differences-communication-styles/.

5. June Cho and Diane Holditch-Davis, "Effects of Perinatal Testosterone on Infant Health, Mother-Infant Interactions, and Infant Development," *Biological Research for Nursing*, May 3, 2013, https://www.ncbi.nlm.nih.gov/pmc/articles/PMC 5505635/.

6. Brett and Kate McKay, "Look 'Em in the Eye: Part I—the Importance of Eye Contact," Art of Manliness, February 24, 2019, https://www.artofmanliness.com /articles/eye-contact/.

7. Michael Tomasello, "For Human Eyes Only," *New York Times*, January 13, 2007, https://www.nytimes.com/2007/01/13/opinion/13tomasello.html.

Chapter 9

1. Adam Uzialko, "How to Manage Workplace Relationships," Business News Daily, March 12, 2019, https://www.businessnewsdaily.com/7764-co-workers-dating .html.

2. Melanie Curtin, "Dating Someone at Work? Research Says You Could Be Heading towards Marriage," *Inc.*, July 25, 2019, https://www.inc.com/melanie-curtin /dating-someone-at-work-research-says-you-could-be-headed-towards-marriage .html.

3. "262 Celebrities, Politicians, CEOs, and Others Who Have Been Accused of Sexual Misconduct Since April 2017," Vox, January 9, 2019, https://www.vox.com/a /sexual-harassment-assault-allegations-list. Accessed September 10, 2019.

4. "Office Romance Hits 10-Year Low, According to CareerBuilder's Annual Valentine's Day Survey," CareerBuilder, February 1, 2018, http://press.careerbuilder.com/2018-02-01-Office-Romance-Hits-10-Year-Low-According-to-CareerBuilders-Annual-Valentines-Day-Survey. Accessed September 11, 2019.

5. Adam Uzialko, "How to Manage Workplace Relationships," Business News Daily, March 12, 2019, https://www.businessnewsdaily.com/7764-co-workers-dating.html.

6. Susan M. Heathfield, "Requirements of a Love Contract Policy at Work," The Balance Careers, November 13, 2018, https://www.thebalancecareers.com/the-scoop-on-love-contracts-1918179. Accessed September 10, 2019.

7. Heathfield, "Requirements of a Love Contract Policy."

8. Adam Uzialko, "How to Manage Workplace Relationships," Business News Daily, March 12, 2019, https://www.businessnewsdaily.com/7764-co-workers-dating.html.

9. "Should Employees Be Required to Sign an Acknowledgment Form for the Employee Handbook? What if an Employee Refuses?" SHRM, https://www.shrm.org/resourcesandtools/tools-and-samples/hr-qa/pages/signeehandbook.aspx.

10. Michael Oliver Eckard and Kyra Anne Gates, "Employees' Continuing Work Constitutes Consent to Arbitration Agreement," SHRM, October 31, 2016, https://www.shrm.org/resourcesandtools/legal-and-compliance/state-and-local-updates/pages/continuing-work-constitutes-assent-to-arbitration-agreement.aspx.

11. Jessica Green, "Netflix Bans Workers from Looking at Each Other for More Than Five Seconds and Asking for Phone Numbers in Flirting Crackdown," Daily Mail, June 11, 2018, https://www.dailymail.co.uk/news/article-5833061/Netflix-bans-workers-looking-five-seconds-flirting-crackdown.html.

12. Green, "Netflix Bans Workers."

13. Sam Levin, "Sexual Harassment Training May Have Reverse Effect, Research Suggests," Guardian, May 2, 2016, https://www.theguardian.com/us-news/2016/may/02/sexual-harassment-training-failing-women.

14. Levin, "Sexual Harassment Training."

15. Levin, "Sexual Harassment Training."

16. Studies testing the effects of harassment training are very limited, but some research has suggested counterintuitive and troubling consequences—that after men complete trainings, they may be more inclined to brush aside allegations and discount victims.

17. Sam Levin, "Sexual Harassment Training May Have Reverse Effect, Research Suggests."

18. Hannah Hayes, "Is Time Really Up for Sexual Harassment in the Workplace? Companies and Law Firms Respond," American Bar Association, January 17, 2019, https://www.americanbar.org/groups/diversity/women/publications/perspectives/2018/december-january/is-time-really-for-sexual-harassment-the-workplace-companies-and-law-firms-respond. Accessed September 8, 2019.

19. Sam Levin, "Sexual Harassment Training May Have Reverse Effect, Research Suggests."

20. "Sexual Harassment Training Is Largely Ineffective," Psychology Today, December 13, 2017, https://www.psychologytoday.com/us/blog/evidence-based-living/201712/sexual-harassment-training-is-largely-ineffective.

21. Sam Levin, "Sexual Harassment Training May Have Reverse Effect, Research Suggests."

Chapter 10

1. Justine Harman and Benjy Hansen-Bundy, "What 1,147 Men Really Think about #MeToo," Glamour, May 30, 2018, https://www.glamour.com/story/men-metoo-survey-glamour-gq.

2. Courtney Connley, "60% of Male Managers Now Say They're Uncomfortable Participating in Work Activities with Women," CNBC, June 10, 2019, https://www .cnbc.com/2019/05/17/60percent-of-male-managers-now-say-theyre -uncomfortable-mentoring-women.html. Accessed September 11, 2019.

3. Jillesa Gebhart, "How #MeToo Has Impacted Mentorship for Women," Survey Monkey.com, May 2018, https://www.surveymonkey.com/curiosity/mentor-her -2019/?ut_source=mp&ut_source2=men-continue-to-pull-back-from-interacting -with-women-in-the-wake-of-metoo.

4. "The #MeToo Movement and Inappropriate Communications in the Workplace," On Second Thought, October 19, 2018, https://medium.com/@OnSecond-Thought_27622/the-metoo-movement-and-inappropriate-communications-in-the -workplace-6c593da51110.

5. Sarah Todd, "The New Guidelines for Touching at Work," Quartz.com, April 16, 2019, https://qz.com/work/1595463/is-it-okay-to-hug-a-co-worker-a-guide-to -respecting-boundaries/.

6. Francesca Fontana, "Why Women Don't Get the Feedback They Need," *Wall Street Journal*, October 12, 2019, https://www.wsj.com/articles/the-reasons-women -dont-get-the-feedback-they-need-11570872601?.

7. Rosamond Hutt, "Women Have More Active Brains Than Men, According to Science," World Economic Forum, August 10, 2017, https://www.weforum.org/agenda /2017/08/women-have-more-active-brains-than-men-according-to-science/.

8. Kim Elsesser, "Of All the Gender Issues at Work, Men Are Most Concerned about False Harassment," *Forbes*, January 10, 2019, https://www.forbes.com/sites /kimelsesser/2019/01/10/of-all-the-gender-issues-at-work-men-are-most -concerned-about-false-harassment-claims-from-women/.

9. "What You Wear to Work May Be Preventing You from Getting a Promotion," OfficeTeam, May 8, 2018, http://rh-us.mediaroom.com/2018-05-08-What-You -Wear-To-Work-May-Be-Preventing-You-From-Getting-A-Promotion.

10. Adrianna Rodriguez, "Goodbye, Handshake. Hello, Bump? Greetings to Avoid during the Coronavirus Outbreak," *USA Today*, March 4, 2020, https://www .usatoday.com/story/news/nation/2020/03/04/handshake-elbow-bump-new -greetings-coronavirus-outbreak/4937302002/;
Yuki Noguchi, "Nice to Meet You, but How to Greet You? #NoHandshake Leaves Businesspeople Hanging," NPR, March 12, 2020, https://www.npr.org/2020 /03/12/814076913/nice-to-meet-you-but-how-to-greet-you-nohandshake-leaves -businesspeople-hanging.

11. Shannon Firth, "Could the 'Pence Effect' Undo #MeToo?" MedpageToday, March 7, 2019, https://www.medpagetoday.com/publichealthpolicy/generalprofessional issues/78432.

Chapter 11

1. Andrew Welsch, "Merrill Employee Sues Firm over Sexual Harassment, Discrimination," OnWallStreet, August 20, 2018, https://onwallstreet.financial-planning.com /news/merrill-lynch-employee-sues-firm-over-sexual-harassment-discrimination.

2. "Remembering Names," Dale Carnegie, https://www.dalecarnegie.com/en /courses/remember-names-new-jersey-northern-classroom.

Chapter 12

1. Michael Alison Chandler, "Men Account for Nearly 1 in 5 Complaints of Workplace Sexual Harassment with the EEOC," *Washington Post*, April 8, 2018, https:// www.washingtonpost.com/local/social-issues/men-account-for-nearly-1-in

-5-complaints-of-workplace-sexual-harassment-with-the-eeoc/2018/04/08/4f7a2572-3372-11e8-94fa-32d48460b955_story.html. Accessed September 8, 2019.

2. Temin and Company, "Between Cosby and Kavanaugh—810 High-Profile Public Figures Accused of Sexual Harassment," PR Newswire, October 3, 2018, https://www.prnewswire.com/news-releases/between-cosby-and-kavanaugh--810-high-profile-public-figures-accused-of-sexual-harassment-300723738.html. Accessed September 10, 2018.

3. "262 Celebrities, Politicians, CEOs, and Others Who Have Been Accused of Sexual Misconduct Since April 2017," Vox, January 9, 2019, https://www.vox.com/a/sexual-harassment-assault-allegations-list. Accessed September 10, 2019.

4. Yuki Noguchi, "Sexual Harassment Cases Often Rejected by Courts," NPR, November 28, 2017, https://www.npr.org/2017/11/28/565743374/sexual-harassment. Accessed September 10, 2019.

5. Noguchi, "Sexual Harassment Cases."

6. Noguchi, "Sexual Harassment Cases."

7. *Brenda Lear Scheidler v. State of Indiana* et al, U.S. Court of Appeals, Seventh Circuit, No. 17-2543, decided January 25, 2019, http://media.ca7.uscourts.gov/cgi-bin/rssExec.pl?Submit=Display&Path=Y2019/D01-25/C:17-2543:J:Manion:aut:T:fnOp:N:2284199:S:0.

8. *Scheidler v. State of Indiana.*

Chapter 13

1. Serenity Gibbons, "You And Your Business Have 7 Seconds to Make a First Impression: Here's How to Succeed," *Forbes*, June 19, 2018, https://www.forbes.com/sites/serenitygibbons/2018/06/19/you-have-7-seconds-to-make-a-first-impression-heres-how-to-succeed/#b2aae7f56c20.

2. Katya Wachtel, "That Crazy 44-Page Long UBS Dress Code Got Ridiculed So Much That Now It's Getting 'Revised,'" *Business Insider*, January 18, 2011, https://www.businessinsider.com/swiss-bank-ubs-changes-much-mocked-dress-code-garlic-underwear-smell-shower-january-2011-1.

3. Jacob Bogage, "Business on Top, Pajamas Underneath: Walmart Is Setting Work Shirts, but Not So Many Pants," *Washington Post*, March 28, 2020, https://www.washingtonpost.com/business/2020/03/28/walmart-coronavirus-shirts-pants/.

4. Cortney Moore, "Women's Workplace Attire Ditches Pantsuit over a Shifting Job Economy," Fox Business, https://www.foxbusiness.com/lifestyle/womens-workplace-attire-ditches-pantsuit-over-a-shifting-job-economy.

5. Maria Tadeo, "Mark Zuckerberg on Why He Wears That Same T-shirt Every Day," *Independent*, November 7, 2014, https://www.independent.co.uk/news/business/news/mark-zuckerberg-i-dont-like-spending-time-on-frivolous-decisions-such-as-clothes-or-what-to-make-for-9846827.html.

6. Sabrina Kessler, "¿Se Despide Wall Street de la Corbata?" *Forbes Mexico*, April 23, 2019, https://www.forbes.com.mx/se-despide-wall-street-de-la-corbata/.

7. Adam Hayes, "Skirt Length (Hemline) Theory," Investopedia, September 30, 2019, https://www.investopedia.com/terms/s/skirtlengththeory.asp.

8. Hayes, "Skirt Length."

9. Pavithra Mohan, "How the End of the White Majority Could Change Office Dynamics in 2040," *Fast Company*, January 27, 2020, https://www.fastcompany.com/90450018/how-the-end-of-the-white-majority-could-change-office-dynamics-in-2040.

10. Eugene Kim, "Here's the Real Reason Mark Zuckerberg Wears the Same T-shirt Every Day," *Business Insider*, November 6, 2014, https://www.businessinsider.com/mark-zuckerberg-same-t-shirt-2014-11.

11. Omri Gillath, Angela J. Bahns, Fiona Ge, and Christian S. Crandall, "Shoes as a source of first impressions," *Journal of Research in Personality* 46, no. 4, August 2012, pp. 423–430, https://www.sciencedirect.com/science/article/abs/pii/S00926566 12000608.

12. Editor, "Looks That Land the Job: The Guy's Guide to Interview Attire," The Muse, https://www.themuse.com/advice/looks-that-land-the-job-the-guys-guide -to-interview-attire.

Chapter 14

1. J. D. Vance, "Towards a Pro-Worker, Pro-Family Conservatism," *American Conservative*, May 29, 2019, https://www.theamericanconservative.com/articles/towards -a-pro-worker-pro-family-conservatism/.

2. Dr. Pragya Agarwal, "Here Is Why We Need to Talk about Bullying in the Workplace," *Forbes*, July 29, 2018, https://www.forbes.com/sites/pragyaagarwaleurope /2018/07/29/workplace-bullying-here-is-why-we-need-to-talk-about-bullying-in -the-work-place/.

3. "The WBI Definition of Workplace Bullying," The Workplace Bullying Institute, https://www.shrm.org/resourcesandtools/tools-and-samples/policies/pages/cms _018350.aspx.

Chapter 15

1. Chip Cutter, "The Best-Managed Companies of 2019—and How They Got That Way," *Wall Street Journal*, November 22, 2019, https://www.wsj.com/articles /the-best-managed-companies-of-2019and-how-they-got-that-way-11574437229.

2. Sue Shellenbarger, "The Dangers of Hiring for Cultural Fit," *Wall Street Journal*, September 23, 2019, https://www.wsj.com/articlesthe-dangers-of-hiring-for-cultural -fit-11569231000.

3. Shellenbarger, "Dangers of Hiring."

4. Ashoka, "Meet the CEO Who Is Championing Kindness and Whose Company Runs on It," *Forbes*, February 17, 2016, https://www.forbes.com/sites/ashoka /2016/02/17/meet-the-ceo-who-is-championing-kindness-and-whose-company -runs-on-it/.

5. Bryan Lufkin, "The Helpful Upside of Office Personality Tests," BBC Worklife, November 1, 2019, https://www.bbc.com/worklife/article/20191030-the-helpful -upside-of-office-personality-tests.

6. Lufkin, "Helpful Upside."

7. Andrew Welsch, "Merrill employee sues firm over sexual harassment, discrimination," OnWallStreet, August 20, 2018, https://onwallstreet.financial-planning.com /news/merrill-lynch-employee-sues-firm-over-sexual-harassment-discrimination.

8. Welsch, "Merrill employee sues firm."

9. Aoife Geary, "Why Toxic Masculinity in the Workplace Is Everyone's Problem," *Independent*, March 8, 2019, https://www.independent.ie/business/jobs/independent -jobs/why-toxic-masculinity-in-the-workplace-is-everyones-problem-37892005.html.

10. "Understand the Impact of Unconscious Bias on Employee Performance," Salesforce, https://trailhead.salesforce.com/en/content/learn/modules/workplace _equality_inclusion_challenges/we_inclusion_challenges_understanding_bias.

11. Stephanie K. Johnson, et al., "Has Sexual Harassment at Work Decreased Since #MeToo?" *Harvard Business Review*, July 18, 2019, https://hbr.org/2019/07/has -sexual-harassment-at-work-decreased-since-metoo. Accessed September 11, 2019.

12. Rachel Premak, "14 Things People Think Are Fine to Say at Work—but Are Actually Racist, Sexist or Offensive," *Business Insider*, September 10, 2018, https://www.businessinsider.com/microaggression-unconscious-bias-at-work-2018-6. Accessed September 11, 2019.

13. Advisory Board, "How Often Are Women Interrupted by Men? Here's What the Research Says," Daily Briefing, July 7, 2019, https://www.advisory.com/daily-briefing/2017/07/07/men-interrupting-women. Accessed September 11, 2019.

14. Robby Soave, "Professor Who Popularized Microaggressions Says Universities Have Gone Too Far," Reason, June 30, 2016, https://reason.com/2016/06/30/professor-who-popularized-microaggressio/.

15. J. Renee Navarro, "Unconscious Bias," University of California, San Francisco Office of Diversity and Outreach, https://diversity.ucsf.edu/resources/unconscious-bias. Accessed September 11, 2019.

16. "Understand the Impact of Unconscious Bias on Employee Performance," Salesforce, https://trailhead.salesforce.com/en/content/learn/modules/workplace_equality_inclusion_challenges/we_inclusion_challenges_understanding_bias.

17. "Battle of the Sexes in the Workplace," Workfront, February 1, 2016, https://www.slideshare.net/Workfront/the-battle-of-the-sexes-in-the-workplace.

18. Francesca Fontana, "Why Women Don't Get the Feedback They Need," *Wall Street Journal*, October 12, 2019, https://www.wsj.com/articles/the-reasons-women-dont-get-the-feedback-they-need-11570872601?.

19. Fontana, "Why Women Don't."

20. Brooke Nelson, "21 Nicest Things CEOs Have Done for Their Employees," *Reader's Digest*, Updated December 30, 2019, https://www.rd.com/true-stories/inspiring/best-ceos/.

21. Alyssa Satara, "Is Toxic Masculinity Ruining Your Workplace? Here's How You Can Find Out and End It," *Inc.*, February 28, 2019, https://www.inc.com/alyssa-satara/is-toxic-masculinity-ruining%C2%A0your-workplace-heres-how-you-can-find-out%C2%A0and-end-it.html.

Chapter 16

1. Evan Lauterborn, "2020 HR Trends: Industry Poll + Interview," SmartBrief, January 10, 2020, https://www.smartbrief.com/original/2020/01/2020-hr-trends-industry-poll-interview.

2. Susan Milligan, "HR 2025: 7 Critical Strategies to Prepare for the Future of HR," SHRM, https://www.shrm.org/hr-today/news/hr-magazine/1118/pages/7-critical-strategies-to-prepare-for-the-future-of-hr.aspx.

3. Milligan, "HR 2025."

4. Milligan, "HR 2025."

5. Cindy Robbins, "The Role of Employers in the Post #MeToo Era," World Economic Forum, January 11, 2019, https://www.weforum.org/agenda/2019/01/the-role-of-employers-in-the-post-metoo-era/.

6. Michael Schneider, "The #MeToo Movement Has Improved Workplaces—but This 1 Area Still Needs Work (Especially for Men)," *Inc.*, May 21, 2019, https://www.inc.com/michael-schneider/the-metoo-movement-has-improved-workplaces-but-this-1-area-still-needs-work-especially-for-men.html.

7. Tayo Rockson, "7 Biases That Drive Your Decisions at Work," WorkHuman, February 15, 2019, https://www.workhuman.com/resources/globoforce-blog/7-biases-that-drive-your-decisions-at-work.

8. "50 Ways to Fight Bias," LeanIn, https://leanin.org/50-ways-to-fight-gender-bias.

9.   Megan Rose Dickey, "Google paid $105 million to two executives accused of sexual harassment," TechCrunch, March 11, 2019, https://techcrunch.com/2019/03/11/google-paid-105-million-to-two-executives-accused-of-sexual-harassment/.

10. Kathy Gurchiek, "6 Steps for Building an Inclusive Workplace," SHRM, March 19, 2018, https://www.shrm.org/hr-today/news/hr-magazine/0418/pages/6-steps-for-building-an-inclusive-workplace.aspx.

11. Bernice Ledbetter and Michael Kinsman, "Ensuring #MeToo Movement Advances Diversity in Leadership," WorkForce, February 28, 2019, https://www.workforce.com/news/ensuring-metoo-movement-advances-diversity-in-leadership.

12. Schneider, "The #MeToo Movement."

Chapter 17

1.   Candida Brush, Lakshmi Balachandra, Amy Davis, and Patricia Greene, *Investing in the Power of Women: Progress Report on the Goldman Sachs 10,000 Women Initiative*, Developed by Babson College, https://www.goldmansachs.com/citizenship/10000women/news-and-events/10kw-progress-report/progress-report-full.pdf.

2.   Joanne Lipman, *That's What She Said: What Men Need to Know (and Women Need to Tell Them) about Working Together* (New York: William Morrow, 2018), p. 99.

3.   Megan Brenan, "Americans No Longer Prefer Male Boss to Female Boss," Gallup, November 16, 2017, https://news.gallup.com/poll/222425/americans-no-longer-prefer-male-boss-female-boss.aspx.

4.   Cortney Moore, "Women's Workplace Attire Ditches Pantsuit over a Shifting Job Economy," Fox Business, October 4, 2019, https://www.foxbusiness.com/lifestyle/womens-workplace-attire-ditches-pantsuit-over-a-shifting-job-economy.

5.   Ryan Golden, "EEOC Sexual Harassment Charges Up as Overall Total Declines," HRdrive, April 12, 2019, https://www.hrdive.com/news/eeoc-sexual-harassment-charges-up-as-overall-total-declines/552482/.

6.   "Fear of Retaliation in the Workplace: Assuaging Employees," EverFi, April 2020, https://everfi.com/insights/blog/fear-of-retaliation-in-the-workplace/.

7.   "Sexual Harassment in the Workplace Is on the Decline Post #MeToo, New Research Suggests," Leeds School of Business, July 17, 2019, https://www.colorado.edu/business/news/2019/07/17/sexual-harassment-workplace-decline-post-metoo-new-research-suggests.

8.   "Fear of Retaliation in the Workplace: Assuaging Employees," EverFi, April 2020, https://everfi.com/insights/blog/fear-of-retaliation-in-the-workplace/.

9.   Harmeet Kaur, "The Dalai Lama Just Said Some (More) Controversial Things about Women and Migrants," CNN, June 27, 2019, https://www.cnn.com/2019/06/27/world/dalai-lama-female-successor-europe-trump-bbc-trnd/index.html.

10. Jorge Ortiz, "Will #MeToo Turn into #NotHer? Movement May Come with Unintended Workplace Consequences," *USA Today*, October 4, 2018, https://www.usatoday.com/story/news/2018/10/04/metoo-movement-unintended-career-consequences-women/1503516002/.

11. Peter Post, *Essential Manners for Men* (New York: HarperCollins, 2003), p. 4, https://www.google.com/books/edition/Essential_Manners_for_Men/Nm0z610tgloC?hl=en&gbpv=1&bsq=Etiquette.

Chapter 18

1.   Kate Gibson, "Most U.S. Jobs Are Now Held by Women," CBS News, January 10, 2020, https://www.cbsnews.com/news/most-us-jobs-are-now-held-by-women/.

2. Te-Ping Chen, "The Bosses Who Prefer When Employees Work from Home," *Wall Street Journal*, March 13, 2020, https://www.wsj.com/articles/the-new-rules-of -remote-work-11584038840.

3. Nikki Waller, "She's a Couples Counselor, but for Your Work Relationships," *Wall Street Journal*, November 15, 2019, https://www.wsj.com/articles/esther-perel-is -bringing-therapy-to-the-corner-office-11573813809.

4. Harriet Griffey, "The Lost Art of Concentration: Being Distracted in a Digital World," *Guardian*, October 14, 2018, https://www.theguardian.com/lifeandstyle /2018/oct/14/the-lost-art-of-concentration-being-distracted-in-a-digital-world.

5. Griffey, "Lost Art of Concentration."

6. Chip Cutter and Rachel Feintzeig, "Office of the Future: More Perks, Less Personal Space," *Wall Street Journal*, November 23, 2019, https://www.wsj.com/articles/the -new-office-comes-designed-to-please-11574510402.

7. Serenity Gibbons, "How to Make Workplace Tech More Personal," *Forbes*, August 29, 2019, https://www.forbes.com/sites/serenitygibbons/2019/08/29/how-to -make-workplace-tech-more-personal/.

8. Victoria Scott, "CEO Handwrites Birthday Cards for 12,000 employees, Has for Decades," Fox Business, October 12, 2019, https://www.foxbusiness.com/business -leaders/belfor-ceo-sheldon-yellen-handwritten-birthday-cards-employees.

9. Jessica Snouwaert, "54% of Adults Want to Work Remotely Most of the Time after the Pandemic, According to a New Study from IBM," *Business Insider*, May 5, 2020, https://www.businessinsider.com/54-percent-adults-want-mainly-work-remote -after-pandemic-study-2020-5.

10. Katherine Guyot, "Telecommuting Will Likely Continue Long after the Pandemic," Brookings Institution, April 6, 2020, https://www.brookings.edu/blog/up -front/2020/04/06/telecommuting-will-likely-continue-long-after-the-pandemic/.

11. Ashley Stahl, "What Does Covid-19 Mean for the Future of Work?" *Forbes*, June 15, 2020, https://www.forbes.com/sites/ashleystahl/2020/06/15/what-does-covid -19-mean-for-the-future-of-work/#2a0b841b446f.

12. Stahl, "What Does Covid-19 Mean."

13. Akanksha Rana and Arriana McLymore, "Teleconference Apps and New Tech Surge in Demand Amid Covid-19 Outbreak," TheStar, March 17, 2020, https:// www.thestar.com.my/tech/tech-news/2020/03/17/teleconference-apps-and-new -tech-surge-in-demand-amid-covid-19-outbreak.

14. Dana Mattioli and Konrad Putzier, "When It's Time to Go Back to the Office, Will It Still Be There?" *Wall Street Journal*, May 16, 2020, https://www.wsj.com/articles /when-its-time-to-go-back-to-the-office-will-it-still-be-there-11589601618.

15. Amy Delgado, "Employee Privacy at Stake as Surveillance Technology Evolves," CBS News, August 14, 2018, https://www.cbsnews.com/news/employee-privacy -surveillance-technology-evolves/.

16. "EEOC Drops Hammer on Workplace Harassment," SHRM, August 10, 2018, https://www.shrm.org/resourcesandtools/hr-topics/employee-relations/pages /eeoc-drops-hammer-on-workplace-harassment.aspx.

17. Amy Delgado, "Employee Privacy at Stake as Surveillance Technology Evolves."

18. Delgado, "Employee Privacy at Stake."

19. Sara Salinas, "Tesla Stock Closes Down 6% after Top Executives Resign and Elon Musk Smokes Weed on Video," CNBC, September 7, 2018, https://www.cnbc. com/2018/09/07/tesla-sinks-8percent-after-bizarre-musk-podcast-appearance -cao-exit.html.

20. Kris Janisch, "Do Employees Have Any Privacy at Work?" GovDocs, November 14, 2019, https://www.govdocs.com/do-employees-have-any-privacy-at-work/.

21. Eric Arthrell, Jodi Baker Calamai, Carolyn Lawrence, and Alex Morris, "Status, Fear, and Solitude: Men and Gender Equality at the Top," Deloitte, April 8, 2019, https://www2.deloitte.com/us/en/insights/topics/value-of-diversity-and -inclusion/male-perspective-on-gender-equality-and-leadership.html.
22. Arthrell et al., "Status, Fear, and Solitude."
23. Arthrell et al., "Status, Fear, and Solitude."
24. Chip Cutter and Rachel Feintzeig, "Office of the Future: More Perks, Less Personal Space."
25. Jenesse Miller, "Battle for the Thermostat: USC Study Finds Women Are More Productive at Warmer Temperatures," May 22, 2019, *USC News*, https://news.usc .edu/157448/female-productivity-warmer-temperature/; Aimee Picchi, "Why Cold Offices May Have a Chilling Impact on Women," CBS News, May 23, 2019, https:// www.cbsnews.com/news/why-cold-offices-may-have-a-chilling-impact-on-women/.
26. Zaria Gorvett, "The Never-Ending Battle over the Best Office Temperature," BBC, June 19, 2016, https://www.bbc.com/worklife/article/20160617-the-never-ending -battle-over-the-best-office-temperature.
27. Kiely Kuligowski, "How to Resolve the Office Temperature Debate," Business News Daily, May 9, 2019, https://www.businessnewsdaily.com/10964-office-temperature -debate.html.
28. Aimee Picchi, "Why Cold Offices May Have a Chilling Impact on Women."
29. Chip Cutter and Rachel Feintzeig, "Office of the Future: More Perks, Less Personal Space."

Chapter 19

1. Jack Kelly, "Women Now Hold More Jobs Than Men in the U.S. Workforce," *Forbes*, January 13, 2020, https://www.forbes.com/sites/jackkelly/2020/01/13/women -now-hold-more-jobs-than-men/#7ac822ce8f8a.
2. Kelly, "Women Now Hold More."
3. WorkHuman, *The Future of Work Is Human, 2019 International Employee Survey Report*, https://www.workhuman.com/press-releases/White_Paper_The_Future_of _Work_is_Human.pdf.
4. Lisa Marie Segarra, "Mark Zuckerberg Just Announced His Paternity Leave Plans," *Fortune*, August 18, 2017, https://fortune.com/2017/08/18/mark-zuckerberg -paternity-leave/.
5. Dudley Poston, Jr., "3 Ways That the U.S. Population Will Change over the Next Decade," PBS, January 2, 2020, https://www.pbs.org/newshour/nation/3-ways -that-the-u-s-population-will-change-over-the-next-decade.
6. Sam Roberts, "Non-Hispanic Whites Are Now a Minority in the 23-County New York Region," *New York Times*, March 27, 2011, https://www.nytimes.com/2011 /03/28/nyregion/28nycensus.html.
7. Gwen Moran, "5 Ways Work Culture Will Change by 2030," *Fast Company*, February 4, 2019, https://www.fastcompany.com/90297816/5-ways-work-culture-will-change -by-2030.
8. Jacques Bughin, Eric Hazan, Susan Lund, Peter Dahlström, Anna Wiesinger, and Amresh Subramaniam, *Skill Shift: Automation and the Future of the Workplace*, McKinsey Global Institute, May 2018 Discussion Paper, https://www.mckinsey.com/featured -insights/future-of-work/skill-shift-automation-and-the-future-of-the-workforce.
9. Bughin et al., *Skill Shift*.
10. Dan Grafstein, "The No. 1 Strategy for True Inclusion in the Workplace," Gallup Workplace, February 27, 2019, https://www.gallup.com/workplace/247106/no -strategy-true-inclusion-workplace.aspx.

Epilogue

1. Shelley Zalis, "Why More Women Need to Say Yes to Top Leadership Positions," *Forbes*, October 9, 2019, https://www.forbes.com/sites/shelleyzalis/2019/10/09/why-more-women-need-to-get-comfortable-saying-yes-to-top-leadership-positions/#570365b91b0d.

2. Caillie Ahlgrim, "Kanye West Claims Democrats Have 'Brainwashed Black Americans' and 'Made Them Abort Their Children,'" *Insider*, October 29, 2019, https://www.insider.com/kanye-west-democrats-brainwashed-black-americans-interview-2019-10.

3. Patrick T. Brown, "Leaning Out," *National Review*, February 21, 2019, https://www.nationalreview.com/magazine/2019/03/11/leaning-out/.

4. Jeff Zillgitt, "What We Learned about Michael Jordan and the Chicago Bulls from 'The Last Dance,'" *USA Today*, May 17, 2020, https://www.usatoday.com/story/sports/nba/2020/05/17/the-last-dance-takeaways-michael-jordan-chicago-bulls/5210145002/.

INDEX

ABOUT THE AUTHOR

Heather Zumarraga is a respected economic and financial correspondent for Fox News, Fox Business, and Newsmax TV. She is a contributor to various publications, including the *Washington Post*, and has distinguished herself as a highly regarded and well-connected source. As a leader in the financial services industry, she was ranked #1 in sales for SunAmerica Asset Management and has sold more than $1.5 billion in mutual funds.

She received her MBA from the Kogod School of Business at American University in Washington, DC, and obtained her undergraduate degree from the Zicklin School of Business at Baruch College in New York City.

Washington Life Magazine recognized Zumarraga as one of "DC's most powerful people under 40." Her work has been featured by Yahoo Finance, the *Baltimore Sun*, *Forbes*, the *Economic Policy Journal*, Fox News Insider, and NBC News.

Twitter: @HeatherZuma
LinkedIn: HeatherZumarraga
Instagram: @Heather.Zumarraga